Literary Criticism of the New Testament

by
William A. Beardslee

Fortress Press
Philadelphia

TO THE MEMORY OF MY FATHER

Library of Congress Catalog Card Number 77-94817

ISBN 0-8006-0185-8

Fifth printing 1981

9368I81   Printed in the United States of America   1-185

Editor's Foreword

In New Testament scholarship, insights, concerns, and positions may not change as much or as fast as they do in the natural sciences. But over the years they do change, and change a great deal, and they are changing with increasing rapidity. At an earlier period in the history of New Testament scholarship, the synoptic Gospels (Matthew, Mark, and Luke) were thought to be relatively uncomplicated documents which had been put together without careful planning and which told a rather straightforward story. Today the synoptics are understood to be enormously intricate products containing subtle and ingenious literary patterns and highly developed theological interpretations. The three volumes in this series deal respectively with literary criticism, form criticism, and redaction criticism, and their purpose is to disclose something of the process whereby these disciplines have gained an enlarged understanding of the complex historical, literary, and theological factors which lie both behind and within the synoptic Gospels. The volumes on form and redaction criticism will deal exclusively with the synoptic Gospels, while the one on literary criticism will deal selectively with all the areas of the New Testament.

Literary criticism has traditionally concerned itself with such matters as the authorship of the various New Testament books, the possible composite nature of a given work, and the identity and extent of sources which may lie behind a certain document. More recently, however, biblical scholars have been paying attention to the criticism of fiction and poetry and to aesthetics and philosophy of language. Therefore the literary criticism of the New Testament has begun to reflect an interest in questions such as the relationship of content to form, the significance of structure or form for meaning, and the capacity of language to direct thought and to mold existence itself. The volume on literary criticism in this series will be sensitive to both the older and the newer aspects of the discipline.

The purpose of form criticism has been to get behind the sources which literary criticism might identify and to describe what was happening as the tradition about Jesus was handed on orally from person to person and from community to community. Form criticism has been especially concerned with the modifications which the life and thought of the church—both Jewish-Christian and gentile-Christian—have introduced into the tradition, and form critics have worked out criteria for distinguishing those strata in the Gospels which reflect the concerns of the church from the stratum that might be thought to go back to the historical Jesus. It has been shown that the church's vital life not only exerted a creative influence on the content of the tradition, but also contributed formal characteristics, making it possible to classify much of the material in the synoptics according to literary form. Form criticism has concerned itself largely with investigating the individual units —stories and sayings—in the synoptic Gospels.

Redaction criticism is the most recent of the three disciplines to have become a self-conscious method of inquiry. It grew out of form criticism, and it presupposes and continues the procedures of the earlier discipline while extending and intensifying certain of them. The redaction critic investigates how smaller units—both simple and composite—from the oral tradition or from written sources were put together to form larger complexes, and he is especially interested in the formation of the Gospels as finished products. Redaction criticism is concerned with the interaction between an inherited tradition and a later interpretive point of view. Its goals are to understand why the items from the tradition were modified and connected as they were, to identify the theological motifs that were at work in composing a finished Gospel, and to elucidate the theological point of view which is expressed in and through the composition. Although redaction criticism has been most closely associated with the Gospels, there is no reason why it could not be used—and actually it is being used—to illuminate the relationship between tradition and interpretation in other New Testament books.

While each of the volumes in this series deals separately and focally with one of the methods of critical inquiry, each author is also aware of the other two methods. It has seemed wise to treat each of the three kinds of criticism separately for the purposes of definition, analysis, and clarification, but it should be quite clear that in actual practice the three are normally used together. They are not really separable. A New Testament scholar, in interpreting any book or shorter text or motif, would allow all three of the critical disciplines to contribute to his interpretation. An effort to demonstrate this inseparability might be made by taking a brief look at Mark 2:18–20:

[18]Now John's disciples and the Pharisees were fasting; and people came and said to him, "Why do John's disciples and the disciples of the Pharisees fast, but your disciples do not fast?" [19]And Jesus said to them, "Can the wedding guests fast while the bridegroom is with them? As long as they have the bridegroom with them, they cannot fast. [20]The days will come, when the bridegroom is taken away from them, and then they will fast in that day."

This passage appears not only in Mark but is also a part of that substantial portion of Mark which serves as a source for Matthew and Luke (cf. Matt. 9:14–15; Luke 5:33–35) (literary criticism). Its outstanding formal features are a brief narrative (18) that provides a setting for a saying of Jesus (19a) which takes the form of a question and which is the real interest of the passage (form criticism). The question of fasting and the use of wedding imagery suggest a Jewish point of origin. At the same time we see a break with fasting and the attribution of joyful significance to the present—*today* is a wedding—rather than waiting for the future. These features suggest a modification of the Jewish setting. On the other hand, there is nothing, at least in 18–19a, which expresses the church's faith in Jesus' resurrection or the theological interpretation of Jesus' mission which grew out of that faith. This particular relationship to Judaism, on the one hand, and to distinctly Christian theology, on the other, gives to 18–19a a good claim to reflect the situation of the historical Jesus. However, 20 (and perhaps 19b) seems to grow out of a setting later than Jesus' own. Here we see the church basing the practice of fasting on Jesus' death (form criticism).

Our text is included in a collection of stories all of which present Jesus in conflict with the Jewish authorities (2:1–3:6) and which are concluded by the statement that Jesus' enemies took counsel how they might destroy him. Mark may have found the stories already collected, and a predecessor may also have added the concluding statement. But we do not know why the predecessor might have added it, while we can imagine why Mark would have. Jesus' death was very important for him, and it assumes a prominent place in his Gospel (redaction criticism).

If we might call the form of the Gospel as a whole a comedy which overcomes tragedy—the defeat of death by resurrection—we may then grasp the significance of our brief passage in that larger pattern. The slight allusion to Jesus' death anticipates the more direct hint in 3:6, which in turn prepares for the definite predictions of Jesus' death which begin at 8:31, predictions which are fulfilled in the final chapters of the Gospel. At the same time the resurrection is anticipated by the theme of the joyousness of today, which is further deepened by the note of irrepressible newness that appears in 2:21–22 (literary criticism). Our short text contributes to Mark's presentation of the reasons for Jesus' death—he challenged the established religious order—and Mark's understanding of the significance of Jesus' death and resurrection—a new, festal day has dawned offering to man freedom from compulsive ritualism (redaction and literary criticism).

It is hoped that the three volumes in this series will give to the interested layman new insight into how biblical criticism has illuminated the nature and meaning of the New Testament.

DAN O. VIA, JR.
University of Virginia

Contents

CHAPTER

I.   WHAT IS LITERARY CRITICISM? 1
     The Study of Literature 1
     The Traditions of the *Rhetoric* and the *Poetics* 3
     History and the Study of Literature 5
     Interpretation as Translation 7
     Form and Religious Function 11

II. THE FORM OF THE GOSPEL 14
     The Story as a Form of Religious Speech 14
     The Story as Reenactment 16
     The Gospels as Reenactment and as Hope 18
     Jesus as the Focus of Concreteness 24

III. THE PROVERB 30
     The Proverb in Folk Literature 30
     The Proverb in the Gospels 33
     The Beatitude or Macarism 36
     The Intensification of Proverbial Insight 39

IV. HISTORY AS A FORM 42
     Hellenistic Writing of History 42
     Hebraic Writing of History 44
     The Writing of History in Acts 46
     Literary Art in Acts 49

V.   THE APOCALYPSE 53
     Apocalyptic Symbolization of the End 53
     The Book of Revelation as Literary Vision 56
     The Use of Symbols in the Book of Revelation 58
     Apocalyptic Symbols and Rebellion Against Structure 62

CHAPTER

VI. THE LITERARY HISTORY OF THE SYNOPTIC GOSPELS.... 64
The History of the Study of the Growth of the Gospels 64
The Arguments for and Against the Priority of Mark.. 66
The Source for Matthew's and Luke's Sayings
Material 72
Current Research on Synoptic Sources............. 74

VII. LITERARY CRITICISM AND THEOLOGICAL
UNDERSTANDING 75
Imagination and Faith....................... 75
Literature as an Index of Life Style............... 76
The Vitality of the Christian Vision............... 78
Implications of the Narrative Form for Theological
Interpretation 80
The Symbolization of Hope 81

GLOSSARY 84

ANNOTATED BIBLIOGRAPHY 85

Preface

"Telling stories is functionally equivalent to believing in God" (Sam Keen). Both entail organization of experience into some kind of trustworthy order. Some such order has traditionally been presupposed, though repeatedly broken and reshaped by new insights. At the present time this presupposition confronts a challenge apparently more searching than any which has preceded it. The crisis of faith and the crisis of the coherent narrative in our time are closely related. For this reason the present work takes the course of introducing the literary criticism of the New Testament through a series of essays which concentrate on religious functions of the narrative form.

No attempt has been made to be comprehensive. A more thorough treatment would deal with the briefer forms, the manner of their collection into larger wholes, and the structures of whole books. Here the briefer forms are for the most part left aside, though one chapter on the proverb has been included so that the problems of this type of form will not be entirely neglected. The parable, the most important of these briefer forms, has been widely studied, and the interested reader can find easy access to the work of Jeremias, Linnemann, Via, and others. Amos N. Wilder has presented an excellent introduction to New Testament literary forms, emphasizing the briefer ones and the oral speech which preceded them. Partly to avoid duplicating his work, this book concentrates on the larger forms of whole books, though even here for reasons of space it does not strive for completeness and omits, for instance, one very important form, the letter, which has problems not closely related to those of the narrative form.

The positive purpose of the book has been to draw some lines of connection between concerns arising in contemporary interpretation of literature, on the one hand, and New Testament literary patterns, on the other. Particularly because this study is appearing in conjunction with works on form criticism and redaction criticism, both of which necessarily involve a heavy concentration on historical analysis, it has seemed useful here to try to concentrate on relating some New Testament forms both to religious concerns of wide scope and to contemporary issues in the relation of faith and literature. Such an attempt does not imply any disregard for the more detailed historical studies on which generalizations must be based if they are to be solid. But it is hoped that the essays here presented on the Gospel, the proverb, the history, and the apocalypse may focus some perspectives which detailed studies easily overlook and which may permit the asking of new questions.

The present work has benefitted from the criticism and stimulation of Emory colleagues Thomas J. J. Altizer, Hendrikus W. Boers, Jack Boozer, Martin J. Buss, and M. M. Parvis, and from suggestions made by Hans Dieter Betz and John B. Cobb, Jr., of the School of Theology at Claremont, as well as by the editor of the series, Dan O. Via, Jr., and the author's wife and son. The typescript was prepared with care by Mrs. Caroline Mann.

I

What Is Literary Criticism?

Literary criticism, in its broadest sense, means the effort to understand literature. If a work of literature is to be understood, it must be placed in some kind of larger framework; it must be tested in one way or another. Literary studies have used a vast number of methods, nearly all of which include both a comparative approach and an approach that distinguishes between the immediate perception and the reflective study of a literary work. Biblical studies have used some of these methods extensively, and others less extensively.

The goal of historical and biographical criticism is to interpret a work by relating it to its times or to the life of the author. Often such study has emphasized the quest for the original intention of the author as the key to the work. But the author's intention, whatever it was, cannot exhaust the meaning of a profound work of art, which reveals new facets of meaning in new situations. Another kind of historical approach regards a book as a product of its social setting and times and often assumes that there is a deterministic relationship between an author or book and its social setting ("as an aristocrat he had to see things this way"). Similarly, criticism based on depth psychology can explain the symbols and action of a work in terms of the unconscious structuring of reality by the self.

Such approaches, especially the historical and biographical ones, have been widely used by biblical scholars, but they are not taken here to be "literary criticism." This is not because they are without value, but because they have been so widely used that they can be seen in any standard commentaries and

1

interpretations of the New Testament. The same is true of the critical approach which looks for the intellectual meaning of a work, for its ideational content. Like historical and biographical criticism, this style of work has been widely followed by biblical scholars; indeed, it has been the predominant method of interpretation. It cannot be ignored, and even those who criticize this method also use it. Taken by itself, however, it reduces a literary work to a bare vehicle for ideas and overlooks its other functions.

As an attempt to move beyond the interpretation of ideas, New Testament studies have made use of existential criticism, which attempts to uncover the stance toward life which lies behind the ideas. This impressive style of criticism, associated with the name of Rudolf Bultmann, has dominated much New Testament study during the past generation and represents one of the most useful approaches to understanding. Just as it relegates ideas to a secondary position, however, it also thrusts literary form into the background as secondary and separable from the existential stance which the form expresses. This may be ultimately correct, but at the same time premature. Participation in the form is itself an essential part of the reading of a literary work, and, in what follows, the attempt will be made to take form seriously.

Literary criticism which deals with form may study details of diction, rhythm, and sentence structure, or it may deal with larger aspects of style such as the overall structure of the work or its parts and how this structure is related to its impact. Interestingly enough, the leading formal critic of our time, Rudolf Bultmann, has also been the leading existential interpreter.[1] The main thrust of Bultmann's formal criticism, however, has not been toward the structure of whole books, but toward the forms of units of the synoptic tradition.[2] In this book the emphasis will be primarily on the study of the larger forms, and, in order to keep the book in touch with the traditionally heavy emphasis on historical literary study in New Testament circles, another chapter will deal with the literary history of the synoptic Gospels.

[1] For pertinent works by Bultmann, see bibliography.
[2] Form criticism is discussed in a separate book in this series, Edgar V. McKnight, *What Is Form Criticism?* (Philadelphia: Fortress Press, 1969).

2

From the above it should be clear that almost any kind of literary criticism of the New Testament means setting the New Testament in the context of other literature and perceiving it as literature. It means trying to understand the biblical books by methods of approach and standards which can be useful in the study of other writings as well. Many, if not most, of the important advances in literary study of the Bible have come about precisely when it has been recognized that a better grasp of the books in question could be gained by treating them "just like any other books."

At the same time, proper literary criticism intends to do justice to the special qualities of the works being studied and not to force them all into a preestablished framework. One of the exciting features of literary studies of the New Testament today is that, at the point of the study of literary forms, scholars are beginning to ask better questions—questions which allow us to see more clearly the New Testament books precisely as literary works. Some earlier studies had tried to force the books of the New Testament into forms which they did not really fit; thus, for example, the Gospels were classified as biographies. A major question for literary understanding of the New Testament is why the classifications used in traditional literary studies are not very adequate, and, conversely, what the proper classifications are.

THE TRADITIONS OF THE *RHETORIC* AND THE *POETICS*

With some oversimplification one can say that there are two main lines of tradition in literary criticism, using the term now in its narrower sense of studies of literary form. One of these lines, descending from Aristotle's *Rhetoric*, treats the form as the vehicle for a content which can stand in its own right, apart from the form. Form, from this point of view, becomes simply a means for effectively (persuasively) communicating the content, which in turn is thought of as an idea. Since persuasion was the aim of ancient rhetoric, and since persuasion has also been an important aim not only for the New Testament writers but for those who have studied them in later times, it is not surprising that many of the approaches to literary study of the New Testament should have been in terms of this type of analysis. In this approach, it is assumed that, both in the New Testament as a whole and in its particular books, there is a relatively fixed and objective intellectual content, that is, a theological point of view which can be extracted from the form; the form serves the essentially instrumental purpose of making this theological point of view persuasive. This line of thinking fits in well with the heavily theological tradition of Christianity, and in many ways it is indispensable, as noted above.

Within studies of literature, however, a second line of tradition, descending from a very much more important work of Aristotle, the *Poetics,* has been more influential than the rhetorical tradition. This type of criticism regards literary form as an essential part of the function of the work, and not as a separable, instrumental addition to the intellectual content. While in terms of "rhetorical" analysis one can separate the idea from the presentation, in "poetic" analysis the work makes its impact and finds its meaning by the reader's participation in the form itself. An example from the *Poetics* would be Aristotle's analysis of the function of plot and of how the form of tragedy works by enlisting the audience's involvement in the unfolding drama, culminating in a "catharsis" at the end.[3]

This *Poetics*-inspired style of literary study, though it has been far more fruitful than that derived from the *Rhetoric* in the interpretation of general literature, has until recently been of relatively limited use in the study of the New Testament. The reason has been that the categories which developed in general literary study have, for the most part, been formed to analyze self-conscious literary works. Thus Wellek and Warren in *Theory of Literature* hold that literary criticism should deal only with works of imaginative literature and should exclude "ordinary" and "scientific" works from literary criticism; in effect their exclusion also removes from consideration popular literature, legend, and myth.[4]

In self-conscious individual authorship, the quest for effective form takes place in a quite different way from the way it does in popular folk literature, popular legend, and myth, even though the creative author may be unconscious of many of

[3]*Poetics* esp. 1449b, 28.
[4]René Wellek and Austin Warren, *Theory of Literature,* p. 22 and chap. 2, *passim.* Though they explicitly include "oral literature," they think of this in terms of imaginative forms like the ballad and not in terms of the whole scope of preliterary popular expression.

4

his stylistic choices. But the New Testament, though it contains a few books which have some quality of self-conscious literary authorship (cf. the preface to Luke), on the whole quite clearly belongs to the class of folk literature or popular literature, in which the quest for form goes on according to principles different from those of a literary author. New Testament scholars rightly saw that references to such self-consciously created forms as "tragedy," "comedy," "epic," etc., did not help much toward understanding their subject matter. But the recognition that the New Testament does belong extensively to folk literature has gradually opened the possibility of a new understanding of formal analysis of the New Testament. The first major application of this new approach has been "form criticism," as noted above. The new turn has shown that the most useful data for comparison come not from the familiar literature of the West, but from folk materials, myths, legends, cultic materials, and from phenomenological studies of religion generally. That such an approach need not mean a "flattening" or disregard for the specific qualities of the New Testament is amply shown by Amos N. Wilder's recent study of New Testament "rhetoric."[5]

HISTORY AND THE STUDY OF LITERATURE

Through the centuries, partly as a result of the close association of the New Testament with preaching and the historic connection of preaching with ancient rhetoric, literary study of the New Testament has been slow to turn to formal analysis except in instrumental terms, as noted above. Before looking further at formal analysis, however, it is important to observe another factor which has tended to limit the meaning of literary criticism in New Testament study; this is the sharply historical cast of so much biblical scholarship. Especially within the last one hundred and fifty years, the questions about the New Testament as literature which have tended to excite the most widespread interest have been questions about how that literature was related to its history. Even before the modern consciousness of history reached its intense nineteenth-century pitch, the discovery of printing and the Reformation's (and counter-Reformation's) interest in Christian origins aroused a

[5]Amos N. Wilder, *The Language of the Gospel.*

keen concern for the history of the text, and stimulated the attempt to get back to the earliest (if possible, the original) form of the text. For some centuries, textual criticism was a fruitful form of literary criticism exercised by New Testament scholars, even though the real breakthrough in this field did not come until the nineteenth century. In that same century the relationship of the New Testament to the situations within which it arose began to be studied with newly developed historical methods. Again, the presupposition was that the original form, particularly the original form of the sayings and life of Jesus, was the goal of historical study. Even today, in New Testament circles "literary criticism" tends to mean the historical study of the relation between a book and its formative historical situation, particularly the study of its authorship, date, and sources, including the stages (if any) through which the book developed. These questions are dealt with in "Introductions" to the New Testament.[6]

The historical stance toward literature is inevitable for us, and it is also highly problematical. In what way is a work understood when it is understood historically? The force and complexity of this question did not strike many of the first users of the historical method, for they were concerned with the historical authenticity of the records and took for granted that the "original" reports about Jesus (or Paul or Peter) had their own unquestioned value. But further experience has shown that the expectations of these first users of the historical method were hopelessly naïve. For one thing, we do not have a position outside history from which we can strip away the later accretions and purely and simply "get back to the original." Human understanding is always located in a particular time, and what has come to be seen in a work (its history) affects what we see in it to such a degree that we cannot possibly read it in the same way that the original readers did. Furthermore, the prevailing types of historical study, using the model of cause and effect taken from the natural sciences, have tended to explain the past as a series of causes and effects. When applied to literature, this method has usually meant explaining the work by something else—the history of the times or the psychological development of the author, for instance. Valid as such explana-

[6]E.g., Werner Georg Kümmel, *Introduction to the New Testament*.

tions may be within their own framework, they turn attention away from the work itself; for this reason many literary critics have deemphasized the historical-biographical approach to literature and have turned to the study of the literary form and how it "works."[7] Such a shift in orientation is also presupposed in this book, although the importance of historical study is not discounted.

Of course, the mere fact of studying or reading the New Testament at all implies, at least for a modern man, a kind of historical interest. For modern men cannot read so ancient a book without a sharp awareness that this book—or these books —come from the past, from a very different world. We cannot read them as the first readers read them, even when we freshly rediscover them. And with the past so immense, what claim on us has so small a bit of it as the life and history which are set forth in the New Testament? It is evident that a literary analysis cannot answer such questions directly, though it may be able at least to cast light on the cultural role of the New Testament and its symbols.

INTERPRETATION AS TRANSLATION

The relation between literary study and the historical gap that exists between the New Testament and the modern reader can be clarified by looking at interpretation as a kind of "translation." Obviously, the Greek language of the New Testament needs to be translated, and such translating requires knowledge of a different historical period. The past century, with its historical interest, has been a period of amazing discoveries about the language of the New Testament. The popular Greek of the New Testament era, preserved above all in the documents discovered in Egypt, has given students an entirely new view of the character and language of the New Testament. Perhaps the most important general conclusion has been that the New Testament is written in the common language of the day and not in the

[7] Of the many works on the relation between historical understanding and documents of faith, special note can be given to Van A. Harvey, *The Historian and the Believer* (New York: Macmillan, 1966), and Rudolf Bultmann, *The Presence of Eternity* (New York: Harper & Row, 1957). Cf. also William Mallard, "Method and Perspective in Church History: A Reconsideration," *Journal of the American Academy of Religion* 36 (1968): 345–65.

WHAT IS LITERARY CRITICISM?

speech of a special sacred tradition.[8] All the modern translations make use of this knowledge. One of the first of the modern translations, the American Standard Version of 1901 contains what is still the best literal translation of the New Testament.

A further step in translation was the "modern speech" translation, like that of Edgar J. Goodspeed,[9] and a step beyond the vividness and simplicity of the modern speech translation was paraphrase, in which the translator introduces words not in the text, in order to bring out the force of the original meaning. A simple example from the best-known paraphrasing translation, that of J. B. Phillips, would be Phillips's handling of Jesus' reply to the leper who asks to be healed (Mark 1:44): "Of course I want to. . . ." The "of course" is supplied by Phillips in order to emphasize Jesus' readiness to respond.[10] Paraphrase may go a step further, as in Clarence Jordan's *Cotton Patch Version of Paul's Epistles,* in which "Jews and Gentiles" become "whites and Negroes," and Paul, instead of describing himself as a Jew, calls himself a "white Southerner."[11] Here the thrust of the paraphrase is not directly toward entering the "old" world of the New Testament, but toward representing its impact on another, modern situation. In a very simple way the same thing takes place in a book such as Carl F. Burke's *God is For Real, Man,* in which biblical stories are retold by young people from the inner city, and the parable of the prodigal son becomes "Throwin' a Party for Junior."[12]

The opposite course, that of clarifying the ancient world, is taken by the processes which lie beyond paraphrase, namely, footnote and commentary. As these are used today, they serve to explain the world of meaning within which the text arose.

All of these forms of translation, including paraphrase and the modern retellings of the stories of the Gospel, present the

[8]See Ernest Cadman Colwell, "The Greek Language," *Interpreter's Dictionary of the Bible,* 4 vols. (New York: Abingdon Press, 1962), 2: 479–87. Adolf Deissmann, *Light from the Ancient East,* trans. L. M. R. Strachan (London: Hodder & Stoughton, 1910), is still a basic introduction to the newer knowledge of the language of the New Testament.

[9]Edgar J. Goodspeed, trans., *The New Testament: An American Translation* (Chicago: University of Chicago Press, 1923).

[10]J. B. Phillips, trans., *The New Testament in Modern English* (New York: Macmillan, 1958).

[11]Clarence Jordan, trans., *The Cotton Patch Version of Paul's Epistles* (New York: Association Press, 1968). See his translation of Gal. 1 and 2.

[12]Carl F. Burke, *God is for Real, Man* (New York: Association Press, 1966).

original text and its world by simple confrontation with the reader. This is true even when Carl F. Burke's young people reshape the stories into modern episodes, or when Clarence Jordan changes "Jews and gentiles" to "whites and Negroes," for the assumption of direct translation is that the force of the original can be duplicated in the modern setting by a proper adjustment of terms. The vitality of this approach is shown by the response it brings and by the continued use of the New Testament in its various translations.

Yet this limited conception of translation often fails in its purpose for two reasons which at first sight seem to be opposed to each other: because the "world" which the New Testament writers bring the reader is a strange world, and at the same time, because the language of the New Testament has become so familiar that it has lost its edge. The combined force of these two reasons, or of these two aspects of the gap between the New Testament and the modern world, means that not only translation, but also much commentary and interpretation, may easily fail in their task of communication. Men easily fail to hear and enter into what is being said in the New Testament, or else they hear a fragment and transpose it into their own rigid framework which prevents it from exercising its full power.

If the tremendous advances in linguistic and historical criticism do not suffice for the task of "translating" the New Testament, where does the difficulty lie? To raise this question points to the whole problem of understanding as such and to the question of the relation between faith and historical understanding. The urgency of these problems has revived the old discipline of hermeneutics, or the art of interpretation, and has pushed both theologians and literary critics into a fresh exploration of the basic reality, language, by which all understanding is constituted. The issues of hermeneutics and the philosophy of language reach beyond what can be dealt with here, but the kind of literary criticism attempted here can be set in relation to these fundamental questions.[13]

By "historical" understanding is meant all forms of under-

[13]See James M. Robinson and John B. Cobb, Jr., eds., *The New Hermeneutic*; Stanley R. Hopper and David L. Miller, eds., *Interpretation*; H. G. Gadamer, *Wahrheit und Methode* (Tübingen: J. C. B. Mohr, 1960).

9

standing of man in his concrete existence, including the understanding of literature. Scientific understanding works very differently by eliminating as fully as possible the element of intuitive participation in the object and by constructing an abstract model to account for observed behavior. Whether the "historical" element can be completely eliminated from scientific understanding is a question which does not have to be addressed here; the point is that if one is to understand the human and the historical, some form of participation, some imaginative entering into what is being understood, is necessary. The model for such imaginative participation may be either identification or dialogue. In identification, the goal of understanding is the complete elimination of distance between the self which understands and what is being understood. This style of understanding has obvious affinities with mysticism. In dialogue, understanding is realized through an encounter or a process of interaction which never culminates in identification. In it, the unfolding understanding is a "gradual explication of the implicit" through which the "claim of my dialogue partner . . . becomes clearer step by step."[14] Dialogue is here regarded as the more adequate model, though the power and usefulness of the model of identification is not overlooked.

Faith and historical understanding belong together, over against any kind of understanding (like the scientific) that cuts out the element of participation or dialogue. But faith and historical understanding are in strong tension with each other. Historical understanding in the sense of imaginative participation tends to involve a suspension of judgment, a taking the dialogue partner as hypothetical, "as if it were so." Faith, on the other hand, thrusts toward a claim of loyalty, a decision that the dialogue partner is real and the object of trust. This tension cannot be easily gotten around; it is deeply built into the structure of Western consciousness. Nonetheless, it is clear that the failure of encounter with the New Testament is to be seen as much in the failure of imaginative participation as it is in the failure of loyalty. Those who are most consciously loyal to the faith expressed in the New Testament often fail to understand what that faith is.

[14]Heinrich Ott, "Hermeneutics and Personhood," in Hopper and Miller, *Interpretation*, p. 20.

One reason for this failure arises from a situation which the New Testament shares with all other creative literature, namely, that its original impact was made by a "deformation" of language, a stretching of language to a new metaphorical meaning which shocked the hearer (the "dialogue partner") into a new insight. With the course of time such "deformations" lose their newness, and often even their original metaphorical character, and become flat, commonplace words.[15] Thus the very familiarity of a work may obscure its thrust. Even where the New Testament is not very familiar, its symbols and its vision have profoundly shaped our perception of the world; thus there is a certain indirect familiarity which flattens and undercuts shock value and thereby affects our understanding of Christian symbols.

We cannot turn the clock back in order to recover the original impact of the New Testament. We have to undertake our own dialogue with its books and with the reality which they express. In terms of the tension noted above, between faith and imaginative participation, the inquiry undertaken here will move strongly in the direction of imaginative participation. That is, some literary structures of the New Testament will be studied in terms of what can be found in them by the sensitive, disciplined inquirer, whether or not he is committed to the faith which the New Testament calls for. Such an approach can do justice to the element of distance from the work which the task of criticism demands (in contrast to the immediate encounter with it), and, it is hoped, may make the literary analysis useful to readers who interpret New Testament faith in quite varied ways.

FORM AND RELIGIOUS FUNCTION

Literary criticism may fruitfully treat the biblical books in relation to the whole development of Western literature, as is done in quite different ways by Erich Auerbach and Northrop Frye.[16] That approach has the merit of setting the biblical books into relation to some of the literary developments that

---

[15]The concept of "deformation," widely used today, seems to have arisen among Russian formalist critics; cf. Wellek and Warren, *Theory of Literature*, p. 242.

[16]See Bibliography.

have come out of them: Frye produces a typology of Western literature in which the biblical patterns provide a large constitutive element in the mythic structure, and Auerbach shows how powerfully the biblical style of narrative has worked on our literature. The approach undertaken here will be more concrete, however, and will attempt to concentrate on how the form is related to the religious function. The advantage of this approach is that the forms of Western literature have been increasingly shaped by the process of self-conscious authorship, and the standards of literary critics in turn tend to be shaped by these familiar forms, such as tragedy, comedy, epic, and lyric. Such classification has some meaning in relation to the New Testament. A more useful approach, however, is to try to relate the New Testament patterns to their roots in religious functions, such as ritual and prophecy. Such a method has as much affinity with phenomenology of religion as with literary studies, and this combined method has the strong advantage of recognizing that an understanding of how the New Testament forms "work" and how the reader or hearer is intended to participate in them cannot be gained by treating the New Testament books simply as works of imaginative literature. Their original function was religious, and an understanding of their function in their original setting (even though that setting cannot now be recreated wholly—and it is a basic question as to what extent it can be) is fundamental to a grasp of their impact.

The study of literary form is only one facet of the broad task of interpretation or "translation." The consideration of the problem of interpretation in the perspective of recent hermeneutical discussion, sometimes called the new hermeneutic, arose in substantial measure out of the "existentialist interpretation" mentioned above, an interpretation which tries to grasp the stance toward life expressed in ideas and literary forms. The "new hermeneutic" has moved to a broader horizon than that of existentialist interpretation in that it seeks to listen to and interpret the whole vision of reality expressed in a type of faith and does not just focus on the human stance of response toward that reality. It moves toward a thorough restatement of what the text "means" or what the "point being scored is." Such thorough restatement is required to make the thrust of the New Testament meaningful, but, as it is practiced, contemporary interpretation, or hermeneutic, does not always grapple seriously with the relation between formal structure and the "thrust" or "point" of a book. The task of the present study is the more modest one of focusing on some typical New Testament literary structures and of interpreting meaning as conveyed by these structures. Whether, in the most profound restatement or interpretation, some continuity with the original formal structure is required to convey the point is a basic question to which we shall return briefly in the final chapter. In any case, literary criticism can be a powerful aid to hermeneutic, because it calls attention to the structural factor that has to be taken into account in grasping the impact of a work.

In other words, the approach of literary criticism is to accept the form of the work, and the reader's participation in the form, as an intrinsic part of entry into the imaginative world of the work. Hence literary criticism is not as eager as many modern theological interpreters are to move out of the world of myth; its primary thrust is on what the imaginative world of the work in question is. Literary criticism, then, at least as a methodological procedure, has to accept the varied imaginative worlds of various works as valid constructions. Its tendency is toward inclusiveness, toward the understanding or appreciation of a variety of visions, rather than toward exclusiveness, as is the tendency of so much theology.

No writing which has artistic structure can be replaced by an interpretation of it. In some sense, what it is can be known only by encounter with the work itself. At the same time, the work of interpretation or translation is indispensable, partly because of the distance in time between us and the New Testament, but more fundamentally because a particular work must be related to a larger whole. The following chapters will try to show how this can be done with a few of the literary forms that are found in the New Testament.

II

The Form of the Gospel

Modern New Testament scholarship has been sharply divided on the question, "What is the primary form of the Christian message: the form of narrative or story, or the form of address and confrontation?"[1] This is not simply a historical question. The priority of one form or the other is decided as much on theological grounds, that is, on how different thinkers understand the Christian faith, as it is on an analysis of the New Testament itself.

Perhaps the question is wrongly put. It might turn out to be the case that there is no one primary form of Christian speech, but rather different ways of bringing faith to expression, no one of which could lay claim to being the proper or original form. Here this problem does not have to be addressed directly, though, in the final chapter of this book, the implications of this study for the question of the primary form of the Christian message will be discussed. Here, however, we turn directly to the narrative or story form, for whether or not it is "the proper" form of the Gospel, it is the form of the books called Gospels, and we now must gain a better understanding of this particular kind of narrative.

The story has many forms and uses, and a sharp line cannot be drawn between the story as religious proclamation and the story as a heightening or intensification of human experience. The classic discussion of the story form, for Western readers,

---

[1]C. H. Dodd has supported the narrative as primary, as in *The Apostolic Preaching* (New York: Willett, Clark, 1931). Rudolf Bultmann has stressed confrontation; cf. his *Theology of the New Testament*, 2:239–41.

has been given in Aristotle's *Poetics;* the fruitfulness of his structural analysis also for modern stories can be seen in the continuing use of his categories by critics.[2] Aristotle does not intend to give an analysis of the story as religious proclamation, however, even though the stories which he studied—those of Greek tragedy—were stories with deep religious roots. Nonetheless, Aristotle's understanding of how the reader (or, for the dramas which he discussed, more properly the listener or the audience) participated in the story can be an important clue also to the most universal meaning of the story as religious proclamation. Aristotle tells us that the audience's participation in the story brings about a *catharsis* or emotional purgation; accumulated emotional tensions are released through the audience's identification with the protagonists, and thus participation in the story works a kind of deliverance for the hearers.[3] The background of this insight was, of course, the connection Greek plays had with religious festival occasions, even though catharsis through participation in a story can probably take place to some degree in almost any situation in which a story is told.

For our purposes, however, it is important to see that the original setting of Greek tragedy in the festival of Dionysus, through which Aristotle is able to speak of *catharsis* or emotional purgation, is an instance of an almost universal use of narrative for religious purposes. Various scholars have worked in this field, but the studies of Mircea Eliade and Gerhardus van der Leeuw have helped particularly to illuminate this use of the narrative in a religious festival.[4] The story reenacts or represents the primordial reality. The story presents the true present, the present which is "presence," the presence of divine reality. Typically, in traditional societies, there is a story associated with the origin of every really vital activity— hunting, fishing, marriage, birth, death, the change of the seasons—all are understood by stories, and this understanding is not just a description. Rather, the story, repeated on stated

[2]See Caroline Gordon and Allen Tate, *The House of Fiction* (New York: Scribner's, 1950), esp. pp. 449–51.
[3]*Poetics* esp. 1449b.
[4]Mircea Eliade, *Cosmos and History: The Myth of the Eternal Return,* trans. Willard Trask (New York: Harper & Row, 1959); Gerhardus van der Leeuw, *Religion in Essence and Manifestation,* trans. J. E. Turner (New York and Evanston: Harper & Row, 1963), 2:388–92.

occasions (or in emergencies) brings the power of the founding reality into the present.

It is clear that such a use of narrative would be closely related to cult; usually the story is told in a solemn ritual setting, and sometimes it can only be told by specially designated people. It is also clear that while the original subject matter of these sacred narratives dealt primarily with man's relation to nature (as in the activities noted above), it would be easy to include also historical events which founded a community among the life-giving narratives—stories of the migration of a people across the sea, mountains, or desert, or stories of battles won and lands conquered. This is precisely the transformation of the story which took place in the Old Testament cult, in which originally agricultural festivals were given historical content and became the occasion for such stories as the memory of deliverance from Egypt, salvation in the desert, and the taking possession of Canaan. In many respects, the Christian narrative fits exactly this pattern, and the recognition of this fact has enabled Catholics and Protestants to make a new approach to the vexing question of their differences about the meaning of the central Christian cultic act, which is expressed through a story—the sacrament of the Lord's Supper. Understanding this sacrament as a "reenactment" or "re-presentation" of the death of Christ has enabled Catholics (with their strong emphasis on the real, actual presence of Christ) and Protestants (with their strong resistance to the notion of a physical presence of Christ in the sacrament) to find a common ground for ecumenical discussion.

THE STORY AS REENACTMENT

Thus the first thing to say about the form of the Gospel as a narrative is that, in its narrative form, it conforms broadly to a widely used pattern of religious speech. In this pattern, the narrative action serves to renew the story by retelling a meeting with the divine reality upon which life in its various structures is founded. By bringing the remembered past into the present, the story enables the participant to take part in the story, to be present at the saving act. This bringing of the ultimate, founding reality into the present, so that the believer may take part in its story, is the religious background for the "catharsis" which Aristotle and the many critics who have followed him have seen as the result of participating in any story.

The appropriateness of the narrative mode for this function lies in its ability to express the passage of life through a moment of tension to a resolution. The tension between chaos and order is the basic form in which tension is understood and overcome in the religious narrative, but, typically, the victory of order (or life, for in this perspective life and order are not at war with each other) is only a temporary one. Hence the repetition of the story and the cultic act within which it is told; as the power of ordered life wears away, it is renewed by reentering into the sacred time of the story. Thus the typical religious story is oriented toward the past and toward what can be repeated. It appreciates the threat of chaos but understands that the threat can be overcome by the order and life which the story presents. This is true of the stories cited by Eliade,[5] and it is true as well of the function of the Christian sacrament in its usual form.

The structural order of the narrative is what makes possible the transition back into the reality of divine order. By creating its own ordered world, wherein, through struggle and action, an end is achieved, the story expresses faith in the ultimate reality of order and life. It does so far more effectively than any abstract or theoretical statement can do precisely because it expresses its faith through dynamic conflict and victory (including, of course, the resolution of tragedy as well as outright victory) rather than in static fashion. The development of epic and tragedy was the start of a long period, stretching to the present, in which the story has been moved out of its religious setting and has come more and more to express a vision of sheer human existence. But throughout this period, until very recent times, the secularized story has continued to function by expressing the old tension between order and chaos. The imagined world of the story has always been a world in which some kind of order came to expression.[6]

The breakdown of the traditional forms of the novel and the

[5]*Cosmos and History,* esp. chap. 2.
[6]The religious setting often remained visible in the background throughout the centuries of development of the story as a vision of human existence. It is, of course, also the case that there is a secular form of narrative in primitive and sacred societies.

drama in our own time has various meanings and, in part, is to be understood simply as a matter of exploration of new technique of expression. But the meaning of the "disorder," the lack of plot, the lack of resolution, and the lack of "character" in so much contemporary writing is precisely a sign that many contemporary artists cannot accept the conventional pattern of conflict between chaos and order. Of course, the rejection of conventional order is not to be read too hastily. Today, as often, the rejecter of conventions may be crying out for a deeper order and life. Yet it remains the case that the world of the imagination in our time is groping to reshape the traditional narrative form of the story, perhaps more drastically than it has been reshaped since prehistoric times.

THE GOSPELS AS REENACTMENT AND AS HOPE

The Gospels have a clear dramatic structure, moving to a climax and resolution. A study of their pattern does not cast any direct light on the contemporary rejection of the coherent story. At the same time, the Gospel story is a transitional form, itself born out of an acute tension between order and disorder, and it mediates between the "reenactment of the past" function of the story, which we have mentioned above, and the function of moving the participant, so to speak, into an open future. The contemporary reader may therefore be able to see some things about the Gospel form that were not so easy to see at a time when the power of order was more strongly felt and disorder less apparent.

The Gospel is a transitional form, and it is, of course, easier for us to see what came from it than to be sure what preceded it. What followed was the incorporation of the story of Jesus into a history of all God's dealing with man or with history. Matthew and Luke already point in this direction.[7] Luke also moves toward coordinating God's work and secular history, a line of thinking that was developed by Origen, Augustine, and later philosophers or theologians of history. C. H. Dodd has effectively sketched what this overall coordinated history of man looked like in its medieval form, expressed in the art of

[7]Cf. Georg Strecker, "The Concept of History in Matthew," *Journal of the American Academy of Religion* 35 (1967): 219–30; Hans Conzelmann, *The Theology of St. Luke*, trans. Geoffrey Buswell (New York: Harper & Row, 1960).

the cathedral, with the prophets on the left, the apostles and evangelists on the right, the Gospel drama on the east, and the Last Judgment in the west window.[8]

Though such a vision of the "sacred story" would be unthinkable without the Old Testament narrative, it was the Gospels which made it possible for Christian faith to find expression in this magnificent historical epic (if we may call it that), extending from creation to the end of the world, and giving meaning to life by giving each life its place in the overall drama—at least insofar as each life was actually related to it. The Gospels were the key to this expanded history of salvation, for the Gospels fixed the central meaning of Christian faith in a story at the center of history and (as noted above) enabled each man to find his identity through the cultic repetition of the core of the story in worship. Thus the outcome of the Gospel as a form was a stabilization of the Christian Word by fixing it at the central turning point of a dramatic story. The old, old conflict between order (life) and chaos (destruction) is stabilized as the believer enters into the struggle with a clear picture of where he came from and where he is bound.

At the same time, this description of the functions of the Christian drama in the form in which it was expressed in fully developed Christianity (after, say, the time of Irenaeus [about A.D. 180]) points toward a factor in the narrative which has not yet been mentioned—the tendency toward the future. The traditional Christian story does not function simply to reestablish the past, but it also leads the participant into the future.

In the background of this function of the narrative is the development of Jewish eschatology, and the Gospel form represents a mediating form between the stabilized history of salvation found in fully established Christianity and the radical eschatology of its earliest stages. The structure and function of eschatological symbolism will be studied in the fifth chapter of this book, which discusses the Book of Revelation. Here it can be indicated that the original past-oriented function of the religious narrative, which brings the ordering power of the founding reality into the present, functions well when the disorderly and chaotic forces are sensed as real and threatening,

[8]C. H. Dodd, *The Bible Today* (Cambridge: Cambridge University Press, 1946), chap. 2.

but not overwhelming. If, on the other hand, the negative forces become so strong that the present seems to be completely—or nearly—void of the divine presence, then the future, the "not yet," may become the focus of faith. Future-oriented faith usually presupposes a sharp feeling of present dislocation and a powerful sense of the strength of disorder. It was to just such a sense of meaninglessness and disorder that eschatological faith responded, and its typical form of expression was a story—a story now oriented not primarily to the reestablishing of the past, but to confirming the hope of future vindication. The end of the story, in this use of its structure, is not in the past or present and not in any sort of repeatable situation. Rather the end is projected forward into the future, so that the reader's or hearer's participation carries him forward in imagination into what has not yet become real. This eschatological version of the story arises from an intense situation of tension, and it usually expresses the tension between order and chaos as a contrast between "us" (the side of order) and "them" (the outsiders, who represent chaos). But despite the natural tendency to identify the ingroup with the good, and to visualize the outcome as "our triumph," the eschatological symbolism retained also a sense of the openness of the future, which is "God's future" and not ours. This tension between the future as a projection of "our success" and the future as openness accounts for much of the "stretched," tense nature of the eschatological symbols.

On the whole, the Gospels represent a strong thrust toward presenting the future as "openness," rather than a "projection of ourselves," even though they also, in keeping with this type of symbolism, emphasize strongly the rightness of the ingroup as well. Openness is suggested by the negative symbols that so often appear with respect to the future: "To sit at my right hand or at my left is not mine to grant"; "They neither marry nor are given in marriage"; "Of that day or that hour no one knows, not even the angels in heaven, nor the Son."[9] Unlike the typical apocalyptic book which expends great imaginative effort to visualize the future, the Gospels are strikingly lacking in this symbolization. But they are strongly eschatological in being documents of hope. The movement toward the future is

[9] Mark 10:40; Mark 12:25; Mark 13:32.

most clearly revealed in the way these books come to an end—the "end" of the book does not simply bring the "plot" to a conclusion which resolves the action, though there is a sense in which this takes place. More profoundly, however, the ending—the story of resurrection conveyed through the disciples' discovery of the empty tomb—shows that the story does not end with the ending of the book; rather the Gospel narrative is a story of how something began that is still in process and moving toward its future and conclusion.

One of the ways in which the Gospels show themselves to be mediating forms is their presentation of the future toward which they move as both in the world and beyond the world. Matthew and Luke make the "in the world" dimension of the future more explicit,[10] but it is already implicit in Mark.[11] However, Mark's reserve about the appearances of the risen Lord[12] suggests more sharply that the future into which the reader or hearer is led is the transcendent future; that is, the absence of the resurrected Christ's appearances in this world suggests that the "end" which one faces is a mystery.

One characteristic of the Gospel form is thus its combination of two distinct functions of religious narrative: the reenactment of the past and the leading into the future. But very often in religious narrative these functions are carried out in quite general terms, or, put otherwise, mythologically. There is a large mythological or general component in the Gospels, but a contrasting feature of the Gospel type, and one which has been of immense influence in both theology and literature, is the way in which these books grapple with the issues of life in terms of concrete personal existences. Part of the reason for this is built into the eschatological tradition from which they arise, for the shift from past-oriented narrative to future-oriented, noted above, arose from a discontent with present reality that sprang partly from an increasing sense of the problematic of the individual's existence. One of the meanings of the new apocalyptic faith in the resurrection of the dead is

[10]See above, note 7.
[11]James M. Robinson, *The Problem of History in Mark* (London: S.C.M. Press, 1957), pp. 59–60.
[12]This presupposes that Mark was intended to end abruptly at Mark 16:8, and that the author did not include a description of the appearance of the risen Lord, probably because the appearances, to him, belonged to a "different world" from the world he presented in his Gospel.

an affirmation of the importance of the individual, concrete existence. The anxiety aroused by the fact that there are so few who are saved is a related expression of this concern.[13] Most apocalyptic literature remained content with generalized or mythological ways of speaking of concrete existence; only in the Gospels has the concrete particularity of existence received such powerful expression.

Erich Auerbach, in his important study, *Mimesis,* has chosen the story of Peter's denial to show the method of the Gospel writers at work in this regard.[14] He contrasts this story with two pieces of ancient writing produced in Hellenistic-Roman culture. They are selections from Petronius's *Banquet* (37 f.) and from Tacitus's *Histories* (I.16 f.). By analyzing these sections, Auerbach shows that the ancient tradition of the separation of tragic and comic styles was much more than a stylistic convention, and that it expressed a pervasive understanding of reality which prevented both Petronius and Tacitus from taking their common people seriously as vehicles for actual historical transformation. Peter, on the other hand, in Mark's narrative, is engaged in a situation which "sets man's whole world astir,"[15] which involves the ordinary concrete individual in an emerging historical process and does not reserve serious significance exclusively for the exalted person. Auerbach's whole treatment deserves to be read in its own right, particularly for the way in which he shows how long it took the new ground broken by the Hebraic-Christian tradition to be mastered by literary art—not until Dante was there a thorough bringing together of the two styles. Auerbach may wrongly think that this particular narrative is more historically accurate than it really is, when he says that Peter's "personal account may be assumed to have been the basis of the story."[16] But the degree of historical factuality is not the central question. The important thing is the mode of presenting reality. Here Auerbach has put all subsequent students deeply in his debt by showing how profoundly the presentation of reality in later literature is stimulated by the possibilities opened up in such

[13] 2 Esdras 8:1.
[14] Erich Auerbach, *Mimesis,* pp. 20–43.
[15] *Ibid.,* p. 37.
[16] *Ibid.,* p. 36. On the nature of this story, see Rudolf Bultmann, *The History of the Synoptic Tradition,* pp. 269–78.

a story as that of Peter's denial or by Auerbach's Old Testament example of the story of Abraham's sacrifice of Isaac. Tracing the thread of Peter's destiny as it is narrated in the Gospels, Auerbach shows how the presentation of Peter embodies tragic depth and significance, even though Peter is an ordinary person and is presented in the ordinary, "popular" style. He comments:

A tragic figure from such a background, a hero of such weakness, who yet derives the highest force from his very weakness, such a to and fro of the pendulum, is incompatible with the sublime style of classical antique literature. . . . What we see here is a world which, on the one hand is entirely real, average, identifiable as to time and place, but which on the other hand is shaken in its very foundations, is transforming and renewing itself before our very eyes.[17]

Auerbach goes on to comment that the history in question which is coming into being "progresses to somewhere outside of history, to the end of time or the coincidence of all times,"[18] yet from his point of view, what is important is the fact that the concrete ordinary person is presented with utmost seriousness and is taken seriously, not just as an isolated individual, but as a participant in the unfolding historical reality which compels men's reaction one way or another.

The above quotation, which shows what a student of literature identifies as centrally significant in the Gospel form, is worthy of close attention in many respects. It is evident that the aspect of orientation toward an ultimate end is not of primary importance for Auerbach. What he concentrates upon is the ability of this form of narrative to endow the life of the ordinary person with ultimate seriousness. The stylistic device which is appropriate for this purpose Auerbach finds to be the usual form of popular, nonliterary narrative: direct discourse which takes place between Peter and the serving girl: "But here—in the scene of Peter's denial—the dramatic tension of the moment when the actors stand face to face has been given a salience and immediacy compared with which the dialogue (stichomythy) of antique tragedy appears highly stylized."[19]

[17]Ibid., pp. 37–38.
[18]Ibid., p. 39.
[19]Ibid., p. 40.

JESUS AS THE FOCUS OF CONCRETENESS

Auerbach chooses for his example from the Gospels the figure of Peter, who is, apart from Jesus, the most fully realized figure in the narrative. Obviously, however, it is in the presentation of the figure of Jesus that the key to the concreteness and depth of the Gospel lies. This concreteness is not achieved by resorting to the techniques of biography or history as they were practiced in ancient times. The materials remain popular or nonliterary materials, in which the person is presented through the individual incident rather than through an organized total structure. The overall outline of Jesus' work is created by putting him in the framework of a story of deliverance, a story that, as noted above, expresses both past-oriented reenactment and future-oriented hope. The materials which went into the story were quite varied.[20] Some types were already little narratives—miracle stories or stories which climax in confrontation with a saying of Jesus (apophthegms). Another basic type is the parable, which has a narrative element but in which Jesus is the narrator, not a participant in the story.[21] In others, particularly the material from Q, narrative is quite subsidiary or absent. The Sermon on the Mount will serve as an example.[22] For the most part, the connections between these short narratives or sayings are quite loose. What counts in the Gospel form as a whole is their cumulative effect. Cumulative repetition, rather than historical development or surprise, is the way in which these many short stories and sayings prepare for the great climax of the Gospel. The attempt to read out of Mark or the other Gospels a coherent historical development, for instance a history of early successes and then gradual alienation, fails, since the books were not written for the purpose of collecting data on the historical development. There is a dramatic structure to the story as a whole, and the element of surprise is often present in the way in which the individual stories overturn conventional judgments about God or about goodness, but surprise is not an

[20]On these and on the principles of their assemblage, see McKnight, *What Is Form Criticism?*, and Bultmann, *History of the Synoptic Tradition.*
[21]Cf. Dan O. Via, Jr., *The Parables,* for a treatment of the parables from the point of view of literary criticism.
[22]See chap. 3, on the proverb.

element in the overall effect of the pattern. Rather, the repetition of the same sort of thing again and again emphasizes the inevitability of the outcome. The use of repetition to dramatize the inevitability of the outcome is even more apparent in the plan of the Gospel of John.

What is distinctive about the Gospel form as a story of salvation is the way in which, both in the shorter units and in the passion story, which is the key to their meaning, everything centers on Jesus, who is the vehicle of the kingdom of God. Most modern discussions of this point, namely, that the Gospels center on Jesus, have turned on the question of the historical accuracy of their reporting. We shall set this question aside in order to study the dramatic concentration on the figure of Jesus, noting only that, as Helmut Koester observes, the issue is not the quantity of historically accurate material, but the extent to which the earthly Jesus functioned as a norm.[23]

The Gospels are not all alike. Mark provides the model and best fits the definition of Martin Kähler: a passion narrative with an extended introduction. The most striking feature of this introduction is a series of "signs," probably taken from an earlier source. By making the messiahship of Jesus secret, Mark has made these signs mysterious rather than direct manifestations of Jesus' power. Luke, in contrast, understands the manifestation of Jesus' power as much less ambiguous and comes closer to portraying Jesus as a "divine man" of the Hellenistic type. One of the creative frontiers of New Testament scholarship today is the effort to clarify both the distinctive features of each Gospel writer and the nature of his sources.[24] These problems are discussed elsewhere.[25] Here we must risk looking in a more general way at the narrative form, despite the differences between Mark and Luke, and without regard to the special problems of Matthew.

In an important article, Hans W. Frei has sketched the dra-

[23]Helmut Koester, "One Jesus and Four Primitive Gospels," p. 205, with reference to a prior formulation by Ernst Käsemann.
[24]See Koester, "One Jesus and Four Primitive Gospels," and James M. Robinson, "Kerygma and History in the New Testament," in J. Philip Hyatt, ed., The Bible in Modern Scholarship (New York: Abingdon Press, 1965), esp. pp. 131–46.
[25]See Norman Perrin, What Is Redaction Criticism? (Philadelphia: Fortress Press, 1969).

matic structure of the Gospel, relying mainly on Luke.[26] He shows how the selfhood of Jesus increasingly bears the whole weight of the action as the story progresses: at the beginning, Jesus is identified with Israel; it is the promises and hopes of Israel which give him direction. Then in a large portion of the story, Jesus is the instrument through which God brings his kingdom; finally, when he sets his face to Jerusalem, "the figure of Jesus emerges more and more as one whose mission it is to enact his singular destiny, while the kingdom of God and the Son of Man who embodies it with its authority fade into the background."[27] The stress on Jesus as an individual carries over into the Lucan resurrection stories, about which Frei says, ". . . just at the point where the divine activity reaches its climax in God's resurrecting action it is Jesus and not God who is manifest as the presence of God."[28]

What is taking place here is the concretization of myth, a concretization impelled by the transposition of the future into the present, which is an essential part of the Gospel process. The humanization of the story has gone farther in Luke than in Mark, as Amos N. Wilder properly reminds Frei in a comment on his article.[29] In the earliest written form of the Gospel narrative, the Marcan form, the resurrected Christ does not concretely appear in the final, climactic scene. This is because Mark was interested in another kind of evidence—the presence of the living Lord in the believing community. But the earthly Jesus of Mark has the same concrete traits that Frei sees in Luke.

To say that the Gospel form is the concretization of myth does not mean that the Gospels are completely unhistorical. There were memories of Jesus which were a basic ingredient of the Gospel tradition, though these memories were modified and supplemented drastically in the one to two generations which passed between the time of Jesus and the time of the writing of the Gospels.[30] The existence of memories, however,

[26]Hans W. Frei, "Theological Reflections on the Gospel Accounts of Jesus' Death and Resurrection," *The Christian Scholar* 49 (1965–66): 263–306, esp. 292–97.
[27]*Ibid.*, p. 295.
[28]*Ibid.*, p. 296.
[29]Amos N. Wilder, "Comment," *The Christian Scholar* 49 (1966):307–9.
[30]See Norman O. Perrin, *Rediscovering the Teaching of Jesus* (New York: Harper & Row, 1966).

does not account for the Gospel form, for even though the memories of Jesus were very powerful ones, there were memories of many other striking persons as well. Rather, as Frei points out, the whole weight of destiny expressed in the faith of Israel and in the eschatological hope has come to rest on one figure. Dramatically this is powerfully expressed in the increasing concentration on Jesus which the Gospel story shows as it progresses toward its end.

The concentration of the story on Jesus is closely related to the pressure on the narrative form which is brought about by the shift from past-orientation to future-orientation. The original function of the story in a religious setting, the function of recapitulation or reenactment, is fulfilled by the Gospels as shown above; indeed it is not too much to say that this function was reestablished in Christianity by the Gospels, or at least by the same movement of faith which produced the Gospels. This function requires a story which comes to an end, so that the reentry into the sacred realm can be repeated again and again. But an eschatological story does not come to an end in this sense—it is unfinished, allusive, pointing to the unknown future either in the negative symbols predominantly characteristic of the Gospels or the analogical symbols so familiar in other eschatological literature (fruitfulness of the earth, peace, the rule of justice, etc.). It is by its power to present the "not yet," the end that has not yet come, that the eschatological narrative lives.

The Gospels combine these two styles of religious speech, the style of reenactment and the style of imaginative carrying-forward into the future, and what distinguishes them from the usual eschatological style is the tension in them between the fulfillment of God's eschatological reign in Jesus and the unfulfilled hope: the resurrection of Christ, which has already taken place and is an event in the past, is a "future-event," a disclosure of the future. But it is a disclosure which does not transform reality; in one sense the resurrection is the dawning of a new age, and in another sense nothing is changed and everything goes on as before. This paradox of the new-in-old finds concrete expression in the synoptic Gospels in the figure of Jesus. The concreteness of his story has its roots in the early Christian proclamation of Jesus' death and resurrection.

The particularity of his death insured that, as this proclamation became the basis of the synoptic narratives, Jesus would
not be dissolved into a "divine man" with typical, but not concrete, features. Stories about Jesus were then selected to dramatize what is meant by death and resurrection, life through
death, the new in the old. The whole process was further
grounded in the memory of Jesus' own parables, which interweave the particular and the everyday with the new and un-
expected.[31] To set this insight about the Gospel pattern into
relation to the history of Western literature as sketched by
Auerbach, one could say that it required the apprehension of
the kingdom of God occurring in a concrete human life in
order to bring to consciousness and to literary expression the
selfhood of the ordinary individual as the bearer of destiny.[32]

If this is correct, there is a closer connection than appears
on the surface between the breakup of coherent narrative in
contemporary fiction and the transitional narrative of the Gospels. Though the Gospels are strongly coherent narratives, and
though they function as religious narratives to reenact the point
of origin, the Gospels have in them a strong eschatological-
revolutionary component that rebels against order imposed
from the past. This element is most visible in Mark; both
Matthew and Luke impose the familiar pattern of order in the
world more strongly than does Mark. Later Christians carried
the process of integrating Christian faith into familiar patterns
of worldly order even farther. By observing this steady line of
development, some students of the New Testament who are
sympathetic to the revolutionary-eschatological temper have
concluded that eschatology is fundamentally at war with any
pattern of order, and that if we could get back to the earliest
stage of Christianity, we would find pure, spontaneous freedom
rather than any kind of order as the meaning of faith. But
though the waning of eschatological tension that can be seen
in the development of the Gospel pattern did go hand in hand
with an increase of familiar forms of order, that does not mean
that the original eschatology could live without structure. In

[31]See Wilder, *Language of the Gospel*, chap. 5.
[32]For an exploration of literary concreteness in relation to the figure of
Christ, see Christine Downing, "Typology and the Literary Christ Figure," *Journal of the American Academy of Religion* 36 (1968): 13–27.

fact, it was by being incorporated into a structure, in this case a narrative structure, that eschatology was enabled to have a continuing impact. It was the centering of imagination on the concrete figure of Jesus which prevented the revolutionary-eschatological dimension of faith from thrusting toward a total dissolution of order. The bearing of this insight on contemporary eschatological style will be explored further in chapter five on the apocalyptic form.

III

The Proverb

THE PROVERB IN FOLK LITERATURE

Proverbial forms of speech have come into special prominence again in our own time, and for reasons not unrelated to the breakdown of the narrative form mentioned in the previous chapter. Discursive thought seeks for complex interrelationships through which reality can be seen as a *cosmos,* a whole. Even though efforts to achieve this vision of the whole were always incomplete and were repeatedly dissolved by new attempts which overruled the previous ones, Western thought from the time of the Greeks has, with few exceptions, moved in a discursive framework which assumed that a complex, but at least partially knowable, real order was accessible to human thought and speech. The breakdown of earlier visions of universal order, and, in particular, today's widely held conviction that order appears in things only as it is imposed on them by the human mind, have resulted in a loss of confidence in the goal of traditional discursive thought. Among the many manifestations of this latter development has been the reappearance of gnomic or proverbial speech forms, disconnected aphoristic statements, often somewhat randomly assembled. In our modern situation, the aphoristic or proverbial form, then, is felt to be appropriate both as an expression of the fragmentariness of existence and of the possibility of imposing a human vision on existence in spite of its fragmentariness. Pascal's brief utterances are an important early example; Nietzsche's use of the aphorism is well-known, as in *Thus Spake Zarathustra.* Norman O. Brown is a recent writer who sharply expresses the view that the aphoristic form is the appropriate vehicle for insight in our time.[1]

In itself the proverb is a form of folk or popular literature. It is prediscursive rather than antidiscursive, though its appropriateness as a vehicle of modern rebellion is anticipated by its long-continuing life beside the more coherent and abstract forms of discursive thought. The proverb grasps a particular kind of situation; it expresses a flash of insight which sees the "order" in a certain kind of happening. Proverbs deal predominantly with the world of man, though what we abstract as "nature" is not excluded.

The most basic form of the proverb is the statement; the proverb declares the "shape" of some sort of situation or occurrence: "A prophet is not without honor, except in his own country."[2] Even the imperative often has a weakened force in a typically proverbial saying: "Do not throw your pearls before swine, lest they trample them underfoot and turn to attack you."[3] This is practically equivalent to a conditional sentence: "If you throw your pearls before swine, they . . . ." But the proverb's function is not simply declarative; its compressed form compels insight. There is an implied imperative in the declarative form in the sense that there is an implied challenge to see it this way. Similarly, the question, the interrogative form, arises naturally in the proverb as a part of its function of compelling or challenging insight: "Which of you by being anxious can add one cubit to his span of life?"[4]

Thus the proverb functions in a much less abstract and a much less unified world than the world to which traditional discursive thought is reaching out. At the same time, the function of the proverb in ancient times was much more positively related to what was emerging as systematic and discursive thought than is the case with a Nietzsche or a Norman O. Brown. In the ancient setting the proverb represented an ordering of a particular bit of experience. It is a

[1] See Norman O. Brown, *Love's Body* (New York: Random House, 1966), and Norman O. Brown, "Apocalypse: The Place of Mystery in the Life of the Mind," in Hopper and Miller, eds., *Interpretation*, pp. 7–13.
[2] Mark 6:4.
[3] Matt. 7:6.
[4] Matt. 6:27.

tract of experience which can be repeated. That is the whole point of the proverb, which by its nature cannot deal with a unique situation. And it is an orderly tract of experience; that is the reason for the declarative form. Things are that way. Indeed, some transaction, some process is usually implied in the proverb. In this sense, though it is not in any way a narrative, it implies a story, something, in fact, that happens, that moves through a sequence in a way which can be known. Thus in spite of its long life alongside of discursive thought, it is correct to regard the proverb historically as a step on the way toward a systematic view of reality, just as the myth can in its own way be so regarded even though it also lived on alongside of systematic thought for a long time.

In the ancient Near East, the proverb was not merely a popular form, but it was also, and is best known to us as, a form used by a scholarly or teaching class, the wise men or sages. The proverb was not their only form of speech, but it was their typical form, and the proverb as it comes into the New Testament, and in particular into the synoptic Gospels where it most frequently occurs, has not only the functions of the popular proverb, but at least some of the functions imposed by this scholarly class as well.

One aspect of the special direction given to the proverb by its use in the wisdom tradition of the Near East, and in particular of Israel, was a certain generalizing trend. More important for the Gospels, however, is the extensive background of "moralization" of the proverb which took place in Jewish wisdom circles. That is, with the empirically oriented observation of repeatable sequences went the affirmation of a religious morality, a morality which was different from that of the law, though not unrelated to it. The moralistic side of the wisdom tradition had, as its natural point of contact with the proverb, the fact that the proverb is not just an empirical statement; it is a statement related to some kind of human happening. As such, it implies a summons to action, even though the secular proverbs base that action simply on the observed consequences of what men do. By tremendously heightening this "imperative" implication of the proverb and by bringing it into relation with God's will, the Jewish wisdom tradition came to use this form for affirmations that were not merely empirical, but were affirmations of faith in God's just and orderly rule of the world.[5] The proverb, whether in the form of statement, question, or imperative, thus comes to express the sober, and sometimes skeptical, wisdom that observes how life goes and brings what "fits" to expression in a pointed saying. The proverb also expresses a faith in a divine moral order which determines the outcome of men's actions. These two motifs of wisdom were thoroughly blended in Jewish wisdom, as the Book of Proverbs shows.

That this combination of worldly observation and faith in the moral dependability of the world, so familiar to readers of the Old Testament wisdom literature, is not characteristic of the popular proverb in general is shown by A. Jolles's remark that the world of the proverb appeals to us as a realm into which we can escape from the orderly consequences of conceptual thinking, when the relationship to a moral world order bores us.[6]

The two motifs of observing bits of life and of expressing faith in God's moral order were nevertheless held together by a profound struggle to grasp the meaning of life, life here being thought of as the span of an individual's existence. Proverbs like "pride goes before destruction and a haughty spirit before a fall"[7] may be applied to events of longer time span, as for instance to the fall of an empire. But the original setting of such a saying, and the setting which brought it into contact with the religio-moral faith in God's government of the world, was the effort to make sense out of the events that make up a lifetime, the events of a life among men.

THE PROVERB IN THE GOSPELS

It is this focus on daily interpersonal relationships, on how a man gets on with his neighbor, his child, his enemy, that brought the proverbial form into the proclamation of Jesus

[5]On these two strands in Jewish Wisdom, the empirical and the religious-moral, see Robert H. Pfeiffer, *Introduction to the Old Testament* (New York: Harper & Row, 1941), pp. 649–55.
[6]André Jolles, *Einfache Formen* (Tübingen: Max Niemeyer, 1930), pp. 167–68. Something like this function of the proverb can be clearly seen in the Book of Ecclesiastes, but it is virtually absent from the New Testament.
[7]Prov. 16:18.

and into early Christian preaching. The overall framework, both of Jesus' message and of that of the early church, was quite different from the world of the proverb, either in its general popular use or in its moral-religious setting in Jewish wisdom. But a concern with the daily life of man in his responsibilities to his fellows gives the proverb a prominent place in the speech of Jesus and of the early church and gives both Jesus and the early Christian proclamation a point of contact with secular wisdom as well as with moral religious wisdom.

The use and reshaping of proverbial materials in the Gospels has been quite variously interpreted. At an earlier time, the picture of Jesus as a teacher of wisdom was congenial to theologians, and the wisdom and proverbial materials were used to show that Jesus fulfilled this function. Then, with the reaction against liberalism, there was a loss of interest in the proverbial materials. Bultmann studied them carefully, but most of his students have not worked in this field.[8] Often it has been said, either directly or by implication, that though there are extensive proverbial materials in the Gospels, their importance is minimal, since they serve as the vehicle for an essentially nonwisdom perspective of faith. However, it is striking that, from a purely formal point of view, the proverb and the parable are the characteristic forms in the discourse material; the proverb is a distinctively wisdom form, and the parable arises from that tradition. That such a heavy formal presence should represent an accident or an insignificant element seems unlikely, to say the least.

The use of proverbial material varies in the different levels of the tradition, and to illustrate the function of the proverb the level of the pre-Matthew and pre-Lucan discourse material, the so-called Q material, will be chosen. There are risks in this, since Q is a purely hypothetical document, the very existence of which it is fashionable to deny in some New Testament circles. But the review of this discussion in chapter six will show that, despite the critics, the hypothesis of Q is the most viable one.

Taking the Q material as a whole, the striking thing about it is that it shows a closer kinship with the proverbial type

[8]Bultmann, *History of the Synoptic Tradition*, pp. 69–108.

of speech than it does with the more speculative wisdom literature. Arising from literature of the proverbial type and moving into larger and larger circles in its effort to grasp meaning, the later wisdom literature shows a strong tendency to grasp the meaning not only of the little history of the life span of an individual, but the overall history and pattern of the world as well. Such speculation responded in various ways to the increasingly felt mystery of the gap between God and the world.[9] Wisdom speculation is part of the background both of apocalyptic and of Gnosticism.[10] It is not necessary to follow here this far-reaching development of wisdom, which led it to develop more extended and complex forms than the proverb: the longer poem, including the speech of the revealer (Proverbs, Wisdom of Solomon), the dialogue (Job), the treatise (1 En. 72–82), etc.

The striking fact for the purpose of this study is that, while later Christian thought quickly found affinities with the speculative side of wisdom, which was one important source of christological categories, this whole speculative side of the wisdom tradition is of minor importance in Q. Yet it is present and is already put to the use of interpreting the function of Christ. The revealer speech form, "All things have been delivered to me by my Father; and no one knows the Son except the Father, and no one knows the Father except the Son and any one to whom the Son chooses to reveal him,"[11] is the clearest example of a speculative wisdom form in the discourse material, but there are other signs that, already at this early stage, Jesus was understood as the wisdom of God.[12] It may be that the use by Gnostics of this wisdom Christology was one of the factors which led to the eventual disappearance of Q. But in any case the discourse material as it is reflected in Matthew and Luke shows a strong predominance of simple proverbial forms over against the more elabo-

[9]Cf. J. Coert Rylaarsdam, *Revelation in Jewish Wisdom Literature* (Chicago: University of Chicago Press, 1946), chap. 4.
[10]Cf. Gerhard von Rad, *Old Testament Theology*, trans. D. G. M. Stalker (New York and Evanston: Harper & Row, 1962–65), 1:451; 2: 306–8, on the wisdom background of apocalypticism; on the wisdom background of Gnosticism, see Ulrich Wilckens, *Weisheit und Torheit* (Tübingen: Mohr, 1959), pp. 97–213.
[11] Matt. 11:27; cf. Luke 10:22.
[12]Thomas Arvedson, *Das mysterium Christi* (Uppsala: Lundquist, 1937), pp. 209 ff., and Wilckens, *Weisheit und Torheit*, pp. 197 ff.

rated speculative forms. The proverbial forms are appropriate, as noted above, because of the realistic concrete subject matter of daily interpersonal relations with which they deal. The eschatological setting in which this proverbial wisdom is set by Q has the effect of heightening the element of paradox in the proverb and even of effecting a reversal of common sense wisdom.

THE BEATITUDE OR MACARISM

The tension and reversal in Q's use of the proverb can be illustrated from a special proverbial form, the macarism, or beatitude. In popular wisdom the form "happy is the man..." expresses joy at some fulfillment of life, arrived at through the fortunate outcome of some common situation. "Happy was the mother who bore such a son as you."[13] "Blessed is the womb that bore you, and the breasts that you sucked."[14] It is no accident that this assertive formulation is given, among others, the particular content of the relation between parent and child, for this is one of the most precarious of human relationships.

The macarism has power not only to bring a fortunate situation to expression, but even to work on the situation; the word has power. "We declared that she, the wife of Pirithous, was happy, which almost undid the good omen."[15] In this setting the fragmentary and chancy character of life is clearly evident despite the optimistic tone of the macarism.

The declaring of well-being as a word of power and not simply as an observation leads to the cultic use of the form where it is often joined to the corresponding negative, "Woe to . . . ." Cultic use emphasizes the source of well-being in God, and functions within a well-defined community.[16] The Psalms offer many examples of the macarism, particularly in the wisdom psalms, which combine the wisdom and the cultic styles. "Blessed [happy] is the man who walks not in the

[13]Petronius *Satyricon* 94. 1, cited in A. Dirichlet, *De veterum macarismis* (Giessen: Töpelmann, 1914), p. 32, with other examples.
[14]Luke 11:27.
[15]Ovid *Metamorphoses* 12. 216–17, cited in Dirichlet, *De Macarismis*, p. 35. Ovid's example is a quite secularized one.
[16]On the cultic use of the macarism, see Arvedson, *Das Mysterium Christi*, pp. 95–101, following Mowinckel, and Eduard Norden, *Agnostos Theos* (Leipzig, Teubner, 1913), pp. 100–101.

counsel of the wicked, nor stands in the way of sinners, nor sits in the seat of scoffers. . . . In all that he does, he prospers."[17] Here it is affirmed that there is a way given by God, through the acceptance of which life will "work," will come out as it should. Thus the wisdom-cultic macarism of the Old Testament remains present-oriented and world-accepting, as was the popular wisdom within which the form arose.

The macarism in the synoptic Gospels has been put in quite a different setting. In Q the macarisms are eschatological sayings that disclose the power of the future. The form is found in apocalyptic books of both Judaism[18] and Christianity.[19] The old concern for the favorable outcome of a process is what makes it possible for the form to be shifted into this new setting; the "deeds" are still important in the macarism cited from Revelation, for instance; but the fulfillment process has been shifted from this world, as it is now experienced, to the new age. Correspondingly, in both examples cited, the speaker is a heavenly being or voice. Thus the macarism in its eschatological setting is in the process of transformation into a revealer speech in which a divine mystery is disclosed.

It is typical of the proverbial element in Q that, despite the presence of speculative wisdom traits, this transformation is not pressed forward. The beatitudes, or macarisms, of Q, most familiar in their Matthean form, are strongly eschatological in their setting, as the concluding clauses make clear: ". . . theirs is the Kingdom of heaven," ". . . they shall be satisfied," ". . . they shall see God." But these sayings are not future-oriented in a merely passive sense of waiting for the future. Friedrich Hauck well observes, "Thus the New Testament beatitudes are not just intimations of the future or consolations in relation to it. They see the present in the light of the future."[20] The apocalyptic commonplace of reversal, the view that at the end there will be a sharp reversal of

---

[17]Ps. 1:1, 3; cf. Ps. 128:1, etc.

[18]Dan. 12:12: "Blessed is he who waits and comes to the thousand three hundred and thirty-five days."

[19]Rev. 14:13: "And I heard a voice from heaven saying, 'Write this: Blessed are the dead who die in the Lord henceforth.' 'Blessed indeed,' says the Spirit, 'that they may rest from their labors, for their deeds follow them!' "

[20]Friedrich Hauck, "Makarios," *Theological Dictionary of the New Testament,* ed. Gerhard Kittel, trans. G. W. Bromiley (Grand Rapids: William B. Eerdmans, 1967), 4:369.

roles ("the last shall be first and the first shall be last") has become a paradoxical reversal of roles in the present. Those who are really fortunate are the ones who are judged unhappy by ordinary standards, and this is asserted not merely as a future hope, but as a paradoxical present reality. The second clause of each beatitude points toward the future; the first cause expresses the faith in a new power for the present: "Blessed are the poor in spirit, for theirs is the kingdom of heaven. Blessed are those who mourn, for they shall be comforted" (Matt. 5:3–4). "Blessed *are.*" Of course the "are" is supplied; there was no verb in the original. But the sense is not at all "blessed will be." The present is secretly transformed by the power of the future. Thus there is a transformation at work in this wisdom form strongly analogous to the transformation of the narrative form discussed in the previous chapter, where it was seen that the normal "coming to an end" of the narrative was under pressure from the impinging of the future on the present.

Another characteristic of the Q beatitudes is that they offer a strong linkage to their wisdom background, stronger than is the case with most eschatological macarisms. This linkage is shown in the subject matter: the various terms (the poor [in spirit], those who hunger [and thirst for righteousness], the persecuted, etc.), that describe the recipients of fullness of life, are terms that set man among his neighbors in responsible love. They do not allow any "eschatological escape." Indeed these sayings can be read as a pointed reversal of popular standards which valued strength, self-assertiveness, and prudence rather than the stance of the beatitudes. But the sphere of operation toward which the beatitudes are directed is the same as that of popular wisdom, despite their reversal of its standards. They deal with the concrete realities of man among men, and not with some "heavenly" world.

The macarism in Gnosticism can be illustrated briefly from the Gospel of Thomas, which contains a number of sayings in this form. "Jesus said, Blessed is the man who has suffered, he has found the life."[21] While both form and content (rejection and suffering) have much in common with the synoptic macarisms, the perspective is different. No longer future-

---

[21]Gospel of Thomas, logion 58.

oriented, the saying contrasts two realms of reality. By suffering under the world one comes to himself and finds that he does not belong to the world. The Thomas saying reflects a tension between the two realms, but compared to the synoptic sayings it represents a resolution of tension, since the saying expresses a kind of withdrawal into a private community, as over against the "worldly," open perspective which the synoptic beatitudes have despite their eschatological thrust.

THE INTENSIFICATION OF PROVERBIAL INSIGHT

What has been said of one particular type of proverbial saying would hold for others as well. Often the particular force of a proverbial saying can be seen only in the light of its setting in Q as a whole. This is surely the case for the much-discussed "Golden Rule." In many settings this is a prudential saying about how to get along: "And as you wish that men would do to you, do so to them."[22] The saying arises out of a generalization of the retribution principle. The old debates over the "positive" and "negative" formulations of the rule are insignificant; both forms were well-known in the popular morality of the pre-Christian Hellenistic world. But in its setting in Q the rule takes man's own situation as the presupposition for his understanding of his neighbor's in such a way that what can be merely a prudential rule becomes a complete transposition of the "little history" within which each man lives: one must die to his own little history, and thereby that of his neighbor is exposed as the object of true, free concern.[23]

The intensification of proverbial insight is a constant procedure in the sayings material, almost anywhere one looks. "No servant can serve two masters"[24] can serve as an example, for this saying, which could well express a typical proverbial flash of insight, serves in this setting to declare the total claim of God.

In later stages of Christian faith, the intensification of the

[22]Luke 6:31.
[23]Cf. William A. Beardslee, "The Wisdom Tradition and the Synoptic Gospels," *Journal of the American Academy of Religion* 35 (1967): 237.
[24]Luke 16:13; cf. Matt. 6:24.

proverb's demand for insight becomes less sharp. "Common sense" reasserts itself in the textual expansion of the Sermon on the Mount. "Whoever is angry with his brother *without a cause* shall be liable to judgment";[25] "your father who sees in secret will reward you *openly.*"[26] In these cases we see how readers familiar with the "tit for tat" or retributive theme of moral-religious wisdom assume that this must be intended by the sayings of Q. Similarly, the *Didache* reproduces the command to love your enemies in a common-sense form: "Love those who hate you, and you will not have an enemy."[27] The synoptic Gospels do not include the reciprocating promise which the *Didache* has found natural. Careful study of Matthew and Luke will show that each writer, in his own way, anchored the radical proverbial sayings of Q to some extent in a larger stabilizing framework. Both are more conscious of the role of the community in providing some sort of pattern than was the case at an earlier stage. Correspondingly it may be said with confidence, though in this context only as a bare affirmation without proof, that the intensification of proverbial flashes of insight was itself a characteristic form of speech of Jesus himself and that, already in Q, the form has undergone some generalization.

Thus the proverb shows itself to be a very flexible form, capable of expressing very different sorts of ideas and styles of faith. In the hands of a scholarly class of wisdom teachers, it expressed a kind of primitive generalization and as such was one of the sources of systematic discursive thought as well as of the speculative vision of divine wisdom. But in the early level of synoptic discourse material, the striking thing about the use of the proverb is its continued rootage in concrete experience.[28] The thrust of this concrete encounter with reality, as Q presents proverbial wisdom, is to reverse the usual goal

[25]Matt. 5:22; the italicized words are an early addition which found their way into most late copies of Matthew; this phrase is said to have been called a "merciful provision" by King James I of England.
[26]Matt. 6:4, 6, 18; the italicized word is added in most later manuscripts.
[27]*Didache,* 1:3.
[28]On the interaction between general rules and the concrete encounter of decision in proverbial wisdom, see Rudolf Bultmann, "General Truths and Christian Proclamation" in *History and Hermeneutic,* Journal for Theology and The Church, vol. 4 (New York: Harper Torchbooks, 1967), pp. 153–62.

of proverbial insight, the project of making a unified whole of one's life, and instead to call for the putting of one's resources to the claim of the "other's" life. The proverb in Q calls one out of his framework of security to be at the disposal of the concrete encounter. This call is expressed by the use of paradox (the juxtaposition of opposites): life must be lost to be found (Matt. 10:39); and by the identification of master and disciple: "Whoever does not bear his own cross and come after me, cannot be my disciple" (Luke 14:27); "A disciple is not above his teacher" (Matt. 10:24). The rejection of self-fulfillment, however, is itself taken up into higher fulfillment, in the perspective expressed by the proverbs of Q. The disciples bear the power of their master (Luke 10:16) and will share in the final eschatological judgment ("You who have followed me will also sit on twelve thrones, judging the twelve tribes of Israel" [Matt. 19:28]). Here we reach beyond what can be expressed in the purely proverbial form and are reminded that in Q the intensified proverbial insight is given coherence by a perspective of faith which includes far more than intensified wisdom. To discuss the total theological perspective of the sayings collection, however, is not possible in the present context.[29] Briefly it can be said that the form of a pure sayings collection was only a temporary one in early Christianity, except for Gnosticism, which has various "gospels" of this type. The narrative framework of the Marcan type Gospel became, in Matthew and Luke, the overall pattern within which the proverbial sayings found their meaning.

[29]On the theology of Q, see H. E. Tödt, *The Son of Man in the Synoptic Tradition*, trans. Dorothea M. Barton (Philadelphia: Westminster Press, 1965), pp. 232–69; William A. Beardslee, "The Motif of Fulfillment in the Eschatology of the Synoptic Gospels," in J. Coert Rylaarsdam, ed., *Transitions in Biblical Scholarship* (Chicago: University of Chicago Press, 1968), pp. 173–79.

IV

History as a Form

Many aspects of the form of historical writing are already apparent from the study of the form of the Gospels, since the Gospel is an important historical form, rooted in recollection of the past and taking the irreversibility of time seriously. But history, in the sense of recording a story of the past, is obviously most clearly seen in the New Testament in the Book of Acts. In fact, the solitariness of the form of the Book of Acts in early Christian literature emphasizes the originality of the book in using the style of recording history to interpret the Christian faith. This is a style which carries the memory of a community much farther from its cultic origins than does the Gospel form, and one, in Luke's case, which brings together narrative styles of very different sorts.

The roots of Western history writing lie in both Greece and Israel, and the double background of the art is clearly evident in the Book of Acts. The Hellenistic writers of history contemporary with Acts were following a tradition established some centuries before, principally by Herodotus and Thucydides. The rise and, for the most part, the continuation of Greek and Hellenistic history was connected with a conscious separation between thought and action. Thucydides turned to writing when he had been exiled as a general. It is striking that the only full-scale Jewish work we have that approximates Greek historical writing, that of Flavius Josephus, was produced when Josephus could no longer take part in public life.

42

The self-conscious stance of the observer was joined in Greek and Hellenistic historical writing with an effort to explain the course of history. The problem of historical explanation bulks large from Herodotus and Thucydides on, and, especially in the latter, there is a resolute attempt to view history in terms of causes resulting from human action. Thus the writing of history raised the question of human freedom in an urgent way. Thucydides' melancholy story of the revolution at Corcyra is interpreted in terms of a very sober view of human nature.[1] A strong element of moral judgment was a part of much of the writing of these Hellenistic historians. But few of them could draw significantly on the religious traditions of their world. The nearest they could come to wresting a divine purpose from history was to discern an ambiguous and uncertain "fate" in history which was balanced against the "ordering power" (*aretē, virtus*) of the ancient Greek historical leader.[2] The ancient historical tradition was thus rather remote from the religious root of the narrative form.[3] There is a distant but significant connection, however. A frequent theme of Hellenistic historians, as can be seen in the Roman historian, Livy,[4] is the virtue of the past. Here there may be discerned a remnant of the theme of reenactment of the story of foundation, since one of the aims of a historian like Livy was to ward off the dissolution of the order represented by the ancient virtues, just as the reenactment of the story of religious origin aimed to do.

Though Hellenistic history was only marginally shaped by the forms of religious narrative, it was cast in a dramatic structure. On the surface this resulted from the aesthetic aim of pleasing the reader and from the associated rhetorical techniques of writing a cultivated style. More fundamentally, the dramatic structure resulted from the aim of focusing on some great tract of human history as exemplary, as a model

[1]"The cause of all these evils was the lust for power arising from greed and ambition, and from these proceeded the violence of the parties once engaged in contention. . . ." Thucydides *History of the Peloponnesian War* 3. 10.82.

[2]See Charles N. Cochrane, *Christianity and Classical Culture* (London: Oxford University Press, 1944).

[3]On the religious narrative as reenactment of the past, see above, p. 16.

[4]Livy *Preface* to *History of Rome* 10, 12.

of a recurring theme in human history. These historians were quite reserved about seeing a pattern from the beginning to the end of history. But in the shorter run, events moved to their conclusion and did not take place simply in a random way. A particular story moved through its beginning, middle, and end. The emphasis lay on understanding those causes of an episode which lay in human action and which worked themselves out in a particular episode. In broad lines this sort of thing could happen again. Thus the pattern of events as seen in ancient historical writing is structurally similar to the pattern of repetition sketched out above for the religious story, though in historical writing the intention was didactic rather than religious. Some Hellenistic historians were quite careful to give their narrative a structured dramatic pattern of rising and falling action, modeled on the plot structures of ancient literary criticism.[5]

Hellenistic history also had in common with the drama its selection of the exalted figures as its subject matter. The visible leaders of political history, the "great ones," were the point of concentration. It was only in this way that a connection could be made between human nature and historical action, for the pressure of human decision was visible to Hellenistic historians only in the leader figures.

HEBRAIC WRITING OF HISTORY

The other great stream of historical vision, the Hebraic, produced a very different style of history. The tension between thought and action was no doubt present in Hebrew culture, but it never came to consciousness in Hebrew historical writing as it did in Greek. The reason for this seems to have been that Hebrew history was not focused on human action as the ultimate action in history and, therefore, was not so conscious of the contrast between the leader and the observer. Further, in the Hebrew vision, the community shared a common responsibility much more strongly than was the case among the Hellenistic-Roman writers, so that the Hebrew writer could understand himself as within the

[5]Sallust is an example of this style. See Martin Dibelius, *Studies in the Acts of the Apostles*, trans. Mary Ling (New York: Scribner's, 1956), p. 142, n. 11.

historical process, even though he was well aware of the facts of political leadership and power, and usually concentrated his story on the powerful figures.

Rather than as a drama of human action, history was presented as the struggle of God with man, or with his people. The Hebrew historian, like the Greek, was full of moral judgments and much concerned with the exercise of human freedom. But his faith in an overarching transcending purpose led to a very different view of freedom, which in the Old Testament is not struggling against chance or fate, but against a highly purposeful Yahweh. If the Hellenistic historians found it hard to discern any overall pattern in the flux of events, the Hebrew faith in God allowed an order to be seen in that part of history where God was encountered, for, originally, Hebrew history made no effort to be universal and found meaning in "our" history.

The distant connection between some Greco-Roman history and the foundation story of religious narrative, whereby in a dim fashion the history of the heroic past recapitulates that past and wards off the decay of its virtue, has been mentioned. The relation to the foundation story is a direct one in Hebrew history. The great historical narrative which now forms the basic core of the Old Testament arose as a gradual expansion of a cultic story of origin. At the same time, the very formulation of this story as a history, by fixing it in past time, established a distance between it and its cultic repetition.[6]

The order of Hebrew history has something in common with the cyclic order of repeatable general situations that helped Hellenistic historians to shape their material. But the struggle of God with man, as the framework of Hebrew history, opened the vision of Hebrew faith to the irreversibility of time in a much sharper way than was characteristic of other ancient historical work. The irreversibility of time did not mean that Hebrew history was visualized as an integrated, organic process. It did mean that the vision of God's purpose opened the future to the new and to the fulfillment of what God was believed to have begun, even in the face of

[6]von Rad, *Old Testament Theology,* 1:48–56.

painful disappointment. Fulfillment also meant that there was a meaningful relationship among the successive episodes which were believed to express God's struggle with man.

The struggle of God with man was also the framework within which a style of presentation developed which broke through the aristocratic presuppositions of ancient thought to make it possible to take the whole community and its members seriously, thus leading to that concrete presentation of the ordinary man, which has been noticed above for the Gospels.[7]

THE WRITING OF HISTORY IN ACTS

Luke, as he will be called without deciding the question of authorship, took his basic perspectives from Hebraic historiography rather than from Greek, even though in many details he follows Greek models. He combined his history with his Gospel, designing them as a single, united work; and it is readily apparent how remote from Greek historical models the first part of his work, the Gospel, is. But since the Gospel of Luke follows the patterns of an earlier writer in many respects, Luke's own way of writing history can be seen much more clearly in the Book of Acts. In this book, though he was doubtless relying on sources of various kinds, Luke created a distinct pattern very much his own.

The motifs noted above for Greek historical writing are only subsidiary in Acts. The subject matter is not shaped by visible historical greatness; it is the story of a community of faith. This perspective releases the author from the tension between thought and action, as it had the Old Testament historical writers. There is an obvious distance between the author and the action in the sense that Luke does not write as a major participant, however one interprets the enigmatic "we" passages. But Acts is the record of a community's story, written as a confession of faith by a member. Within the community, the ordinary, seemingly insignificant person is presented as the bearer of historical destiny, just as in the Old Testament and the Gospels.

Further, there is little concern for explanation through anal-

[7]See above, pp. 22–23.

ysis of human decision and its results. Luke does give considerable attention to character, but his stories with legendary elements show his intention of viewing the power of the self in relation to the overarching power of God, and not in a framework of the historical influence of human decision.

Character is most fully presented in the case of Paul. Luke combines a great admiration for Paul with a single-minded effort to incorporate him thoroughly into a unified church. These factors produce a portrait of Paul strikingly different from that which Paul presents of himself in his letters. Paul's struggle with himself and with his communities about "who he is" (especially in Galatians and 1 and 2 Corinthians) is replaced by Paul's even-tempered submission to the will of God, for to Luke it is very clear how Paul fits in with the rest of the church. Instead, the thrice-told story of Paul's conversion becomes a model for Christian obedience, and Luke's Paul is in many ways the model for the emerging figure of the saint, a figure who is in the world but continually motivated by a power beyond the world. Such a character engaged in historical action is altogether different from the important figures of Greco-Roman historiography, who match their power (*virtus*) against a chancy environment.

Behind all the details lies the basic perspective which Luke shares with the Old Testament historians. He is writing the history of God's acts. It is true that Luke's history is less of a struggle between God and man than is the case in the Old Testament. Luke's perspective is rather that of divine determination.[8] Here Luke is influenced by prophecy and apocalyptic as much as by the Old Testament historians. Apocalyptic literature is full of patterns of the divine plan for history. Related to a deterministic plan is the tendency to lay history out in successive periods, as can be seen in Daniel, 1 Enoch, and elsewhere in apocalyptic literature.[9] Though he does not display his periodizing as obviously as the apocalyptic writers often do, a scheme of periods is basic to Luke's grasp of history, as Conzelmann has shown.[10] For Luke, there are

[8]"It is not for you to know times or seasons which the Father has fixed by his own authority." Acts 1:7.
[9]Dan. 2, 7, 8, 11; 1 En. 83–90.
[10]Conzelmann, *Theology of St. Luke.*

three periods in the sacred history which, for him, is the real history of man: the time of God's history with the Jews, the time of the presence of salvation in Jesus, and the time of the church. In Acts, as in apocalyptic, the periodizing produces a linear sequence, a story leading to an end. But Luke has altered this perspective so that the end, in a sense, has been shifted to the middle. Christ becomes the center of time, and the final end ceases to be the center of interest, though it remains as a focus of hope. This way of structuring history constitutes a radical metamorphosis of ancient cyclical patterns of repeating human existence. Luke was writing the history of a community of faith, and he did not try to schematize the sequence of the world's history except as it related to faith. He did not list successive empires, for instance, as Daniel does. Yet his vision of a concrete community's historical existence as set in an irreversible linear divine pattern has much to do with the impact of the vision of linear history on Western thought.

Though the fundamental perspectives of Luke were drawn from the Septuagint (a Greek translation of the Old Testament), he was nonetheless acquainted with Hellenistic historical procedures and thought of his work as following them. The introduction to Luke and the shorter introduction to Acts are shaped by Hellenistic models.[11] More important, Luke follows, to some extent, the methods of Hellenistic historians, as his preface suggests. Apparently, unlike their ideal, he gathered sources from only one side of the Jewish-Christian tensions that he reports. He assembled geographic information, though his geography is as much symbolic as it is historical. He offers a story concentrating on Jerusalem in the early chapters, filling in the intermediate spaces in the middle chapters, and then climaxing in Rome at the end, thus moving the Christian faith from the center of the old way to the center of culture and power of the day. The basic thrust of his geography is symbolic. He had a good general knowledge of geographic detail, as shown in his narratives of Paul's travels. Much of this detail also serves a symbolic purpose.

[11]Henry J. Cadbury, "Commentary on the Preface to Luke," in F. J. Foakes Jackson and Kirsopp Lake, *The Beginnings of Christianity* (London: Macmillan, 1920–33), 2:489–510.

As John Knox has shown, the geography of Paul's travels (the so-called missionary journeys) offers a quite different picture of Paul's movements from that presented by Paul's letters, the difference being that Luke "tethers" Paul to Jerusalem to a degree that is not acknowledged by Paul himself.[12]

Not only in respect to geography, but in numerous aspects of his narrative, Luke is at pains to describe details of contemporary life which may not have cost him detailed research, but which do reflect both wide general knowledge and Luke's effort to function as a recognizable historian.[13]

Probably the most widely discussed feature of his technique is Luke's use of speeches.[14] There are some speeches in Old Testament history and in Hellenistic Jewish works such as 2 Maccabees, a book which may have influenced Luke. However, the high percentage of speech material (about a fifth of the book) suggests a parallel with Hellenistic practice, although the speech types (especially the missionary sermons) are not typically Hellenistic forms. Neither Jewish nor Hellenistic historical writing thought of speeches as verbatim records, and in both, as in Acts, the speeches are often directed to the reader rather than to the supposed historical audience. They should not be read as accurate history, but as proclamation emerging out of the historical past.

LITERARY ART IN ACTS

So far Luke has been presented as a writer combining two styles of historical writing; though the Septuagintal background of his work is evidently the predominant one, he works also with techniques and points of view learned from the current milieu in which he lived, and no doubt did so with the aim of furthering the impact of the faith he believed

[12]John Knox, *Chapters in a Life of Paul* (New York: Abingdon, 1950), pp. 51–52 and chaps. 3–6.
[13]On this aspect of Acts, see Henry J. Cadbury, *The Book of Acts in History* (New York: Harper & Row, 1955).
[14]Henry J. Cadbury, "The Speeches in Acts," *The Beginnings of Christianity*, 5:402–26; Martin Dibelius, "The Speeches in Acts and Ancient Historiography," *Studies in the Acts of the Apostles*, pp. 138–91 (fundamental); Ulrich Wilckens, *Die Missionsreden der Apostelgeschichte* (Neukirchen: Neukirchener Verlag, 1963); Paul Schubert, "The Place of the Areopagus Speech in the Composition of Acts," in J. Coert Rylaarsdam, ed., *Transitions in Biblical Scholarship* (Chicago: University of Chicago Press, 1968), pp. 235–61.

on that world. Both for ancient times and today it is a difficult question as to what extent history is literature, and thus it remains to ask more directly about the specifically literary qualities of the Book of Acts.

The question of style is important, for Luke was moving his language toward the style of self-conscious literary authorship. In style of language he brings his work as close to formal literature as anything in the New Testament. Luke's style, as well as his historiographical perspective, reflects his effort to bring faith into functional interaction with his world.[15]

Rather than sample Luke's style, however, it will be more useful to look at Acts as a story. For every history also has to be a story; the multiform experience of everyday reality has to be organized into some sort of pattern. As shown above, the organizing pattern for Luke is history of salvation, a history of the accomplishment of God's purpose. This linear narrative points to an end, a future fulfillment, but Luke has restructured it so that the real emphasis lies on the "middle of time," the story of Christ related in his Gospel. Read on this level, Luke-Acts is a key stage in the incorporation of the story of Jesus into a coherent story of God's relation to the world.[16]

There is yet another level of story in Acts, which works as a kind of counterpoint to the story of the working out of God's purpose. The Book of Acts, however it is analyzed in detail, falls into two main parts. In the first, the church discovers its identity; in the second, it reaches out into the world. The outreach is dramatized in the journeys of Paul. In this part of the story it is easy to recognize the narrative motif of the journey or quest. Unlike the journey of Odysseus, that of Paul does not bring him back to his home. The quest becomes an open journey, an unfinished one. The particular narrative device which highlights the quest theme and emphasizes its unfinished character is the very simple one of the narrow escape, a form of narrative which is more at home

[15]On Luke's style, see Henry J. Cadbury, *The Making of Luke-Acts* (New York: Macmillan, 1927), esp. chap. 16.
[16]See above, pp. 18–19.

in the tale or romance than in history. Paul's story is made up of a whole series of narrow escapes, from his escape from Damascus in a basket (9:23–25), through the various escapes on his travels in Asia Minor and Greece (14:5–7, 19–23; 16: 19–40; 17:5–10, 13–14; 18:12–17; 19:23–41), to his escape from a mob in Jerusalem (21:27–22:29) and from a plot there against his life (23:12–34), to, finally, the grand narrow escape of the storm and shipwreck (27:1–44). This last narrative engaged much of Luke's stylistic attention, as well as the use of a storytelling tradition about the sea. Further depth is given to the narrow escape theme by the fact that Paul's career is paralleled on a smaller scale by the narrow escapes of Peter (4:1–22; [5:12–40]; 12:1–17). In accord with his principle of relating characters by having them undergo the same things, the narrow escape theme is also introduced into the story of Jesus (cf. the escape from Nazareth, Luke 4: 28–30, not in Matthew or Mark).

When Acts is read with an eye to the level of human quest or journey as well as with attention to the overarching divine purpose of sacred history, the whole vision of existence communicated by the book becomes an open one and is released from the theological rigidity which it receives in some interpretations. The firmness of the divine purpose is set in counterpoint to the peril and expendability of its instruments—Stephen is martyred, Peter disappears from the story without comment, and Paul goes through his many escapes to die, presumably, before his plans have been accomplished (cf. Acts 20:25). The open structure of the ending of Acts is fully appropriate to the vision of existence which the book as a whole communicates.

In all of the recent intense study of Acts, not much attention has been paid to its narrative pattern in these terms. In his thorough and perceptive commentary, Haenchen studies Luke's narrative of Paul but stresses only the side of Paul's protection by God and success.[17] Helmut Koester so highly emphasizes the powerful acts of Paul, parallel to those of Jesus, that he classifies the whole of Luke-Acts as an "aretol-

---

[17] E. Haenchen, *Die Apostelgeschichte* (13th ed.; Göttingen: Vandenhoeck & Ruprecht, 1961), e.g. pp. 636, 655.

ogy," a presentation of a religious point of view through the
story of the powerful acts of its founder or leader (a theme
certainly present).[18] Cadbury is the only recent scholar who
has taken the dramatic structure of the human side of the
narrative seriously.[19] The result has been that recent studies
of Acts have overemphasized the deterministic, objectifying
side of Luke's book. But the impact of the book on the reader
arises from both aspects: from the story of the outworking
of God's purpose, as well as from the story of the risk and
expendability of the men who take part in the open-ended
quest dramatized in the story of Paul.

In the later apocryphal Acts, the quest and saint themes
are united in a way that effectively takes the hero out of the
human struggle, and Acts is part of the background of this
later literary form. Luke has softened the human struggle of
Paul as we know it from his letters. But he keeps Paul well
within the pattern of the precarious human quest, as ordinary
readers of the book have sometimes seen better than scholars.
Thus the Book of Acts was able to serve also as ancestor to
the later sober historical tradition of the church, which, like
Acts, kept together the precariousness of the human venture
and the faith in a continuing divine purpose. Whether or
how these can now be held together is the problem for contemporary theological or symbolic interpretation, which the
book leaves for the reader.

[18]Koester, "One Jesus and Four Primitive Gospels," p. 235.
[19]Cadbury, *Making of Luke-Acts*, pp. 235-38.

V

The Apocalypse

There is a profound paradox in the contemporary understanding of apocalyptic. Jewish-Christian apocalyptic is a dualistic type of faith which expresses itself in symbolic visions of the struggle of good and evil and of the final victory of good. For seventy-five years historically minded scholars have been struggling to eliminate, deemphasize, or reinterpret nonapocalyptically the apocalyptic element in the New Testament, for, in their view, apocalyptic is unacceptable and unbelievable to modern man. In the meantime, however, artists and critics have come to speak of the present time as an apocalyptic time and have been using apocalyptic symbols and structures precisely to present the situation of modern man. It would be easy to soften this paradox by saying that the two groups do not mean the same thing by "apocalyptic," and in the narrow sense this would of course be true. Nonetheless, the modern apocalyptic style has important roots in ancient Jewish and Christian apocalypses, and the present discussion of apocalyptic will attempt to move toward bridging the gap between the two approaches, that of the theologian-historian and that of the artists and critics.

Apocalyptic as a form embodies a profound thirst for total presence. "All" is one of the great governing apocalyptic words. The usual style of religious narrative is content to ward off chaos by periodic re-presentation of the life-giving reality; apocalyptic narrative is unsatisfied with so partial and never-ending a resolution and thirsts for the total victory, the all-inclusive transformation of reality.

53

The thirst for the "all," for the total transformation, expresses itself in two different ways in apocalyptic style. On the one hand, the narrative moves toward inclusiveness. Instead of being the narrative of "our" community, it becomes as well the story of "the kingdoms of the world," in order to include all reality within its compass. This encyclopedic direction of apocalyptic narrative may be controlled and disciplined (as in Daniel). Or it may result in an almost formless agglutination of material, including various unrelated versions of the story of past and future, and many other sorts of esoteric lore (as in 1 Enoch). The encyclopedic mode of apocalyptic narrative shows apocalyptic's affinity with wisdom, with the effort to grasp the meaning of the whole of existence, and it tends to produce a relaxed and relatively formless extended narrative.

The other form of expressing the thirst for totality in apocalyptic is concentration on the end. The end is a reversal of reality as presently experienced, and the vision of the end is a vision of the total victory of life and order over the destructive forces. In its most intense forms, apocalyptic vision tends not to describe the end, except negatively ("they neither marry nor are given in marriage"; "flesh and blood cannot inherit the kingdom of God").[1] Even where the description of the end is unfolded, symbols drawn from the present often have a negative meaning. "Peace" in the future is the opposite of presently known conflict; the jewels and precious stones of the holy city are the opposite of presently real or symbolic poverty. But the end may also be symbolized by positive analogies, such as the "holy city," which point to the fulfillment of what is known or hoped for. Totally negative symbolism of the future would mean total rejection of the present.

Symbolization of the end by negating the present leads toward a reversal of basic symbolic values in religion. Original religious symbolism identifies chaos and formlessness with death and the struggle to impose order upon chaos with life. The apocalyptic thirst for totality, however, begins a thrust to reverse this basic symbolism. Present experience is known as oppressive and death-giving, and it is precisely order, rather than chaos, in which oppressiveness is sensed. Hence

[1]Mark 12:25; 1 Cor. 15:50.

the total presence of ultimate reality will mean a dissolution of order, a presence of pure spontaneity. Ancient apocalyptic writing does not carry through this reversal of symbolic meaning, for in it God remains a symbol of transcendent order. But it did have a powerful vision of a total breakthrough not only away from oppressive external political order (the destruction of the kingdoms), and from inner self-contradiction (there shall be no more pain), but also from order imposed within the sacred community (there will be no temple in the new Jerusalem). This vision of liberation from oppressive order as a negative symbolization of the end is of fundamental importance for understanding the modern apocalyptic vision of liberation, a vision which is far more radical because it does away with the transcendent ordering figure of God.[2]

The basic structural pattern of Christian apocalyptic hope was of course derived from Jewish apocalyptic faith. The pattern arises from a breaking open of the essentially repeatable story of origin to make the story which gives meaning to life culminate in a once-for-all, total end. The apocalyptic pattern embodies strong dualistic elements but does not become completely dualistic; the world is remembered as God's creation despite the power of evil in it. Yet the apocalyptic faith could not arise until evil was felt to be all but overpowering; it is the threat of a total victory of evil which makes the faith in a total victory of good necessary. The specifically apocalyptic pattern and symbolism are already present in Mark 13 and parallels, and parts of them appear in 1 Corinthians 15 and 1 Thessalonians 4:13–5:11. The apocalyptic structure, moreover, worked on the Gospel and history forms, as noted above.[3] The vision of human existence as caught up in a transcendent struggle which will express itself in a real history culminating in a total victory of good is fundamental to all three forms, the Gospel, the history, and

[2]William Blake, himself deeply steeped in the world of ancient apocalyptic, was the first to bring the modern vision to expression in its radical form. Dostoevsky is another figure who makes clear the line of continuity between ancient and modern "apocalyptic." On Blake see Thomas J. J. Altizer, "William Blake and the Role of Myth," in Thomas J. J. Altizer and William Hamilton, *Radical Theology and the Death of God* (Indianapolis: Bobbs-Merrill, 1966), pp. 171–91. A useful introduction to the apocalyptic theme in recent writing is Earl Rovit, "On the Contemporary Apocalyptic Imagination," *The American Scholar* 37 (1968): 453–68.
[3]See above, pp. 19–22, 47–48.

the apocalypse. That this same structure can serve for such drastically different books is a powerful testimony to the variety of early Christian imagination.

THE BOOK OF REVELATION AS LITERARY VISION

The book of Revelation is the central literary expression of Christian apocalyptic. Not only is it the only fully realized apocalyptic book in the New Testament, but also Revelation stands in a class by itself in the whole group of Jewish-Christian apocalyptic books, in the way in which the author has made a visionary whole of his materials. Revelation brings the reader into a world, a "cosmos," of its own, and the way in which it does so makes it come the closest, by far, of all the New Testament books, to being what men think of today as a work of art. There are smaller units in the New Testament which can as fully be recognized as having the unity of artistic form which brings the reader into a special world—most obviously the synoptic parables have this quality.[4] But among whole books, Revelation is the only one of which it can be said, "It is the one great poem which the first Christian age produced."[5]

Calling Revelation a work of art does not imply that it was a private creation, written out of the self-conscious individuality of the author. On the contrary, the work has deep liturgical roots. The vision as a whole is bracketed in the framework of a letter (1:4–5; 22:21) not because it has any kinship with the inner structure of the letter form, but because at that time letters were solemnly read in churches, and the author intends this function for his vision (1:3). The book is rich in hymnic materials (4:8, 11; 5:9–10; 7:15–16, etc.). Its action is imagined as a heavenly liturgy. Many of its images derive from liturgy as well, although the attempt to trace out their roots in ancient religious liturgies and calendars cannot succeed in detail.[6] The book was written for use in worship, and it expresses the faith of a community. Yet it does so in a unique world of vision. The early and continuing

[4]See Dan O. Via, Jr., *Parables*, esp. chap. 3.

[5]Austin Farrer, *A Rebirth of Images* (Westminster: Dacre Press, 1949), p. 6.

[6]Austin Farrer attempted this in *A Rebirth of Images;* he was much more cautious in his later work, *The Revelation of St. John the Divine* (Oxford: Clarendon Press, 1964), although even there he attempts to be too precise and definite in his interpretation of the symbolism.

controversy about the book is a clear sign of the special nature of its vision.

In both the Gospel and the history, the thrust toward the end has been modified or deflected by the impinging of ultimate reality on the present in the figure of Christ. The forward movement of the narrative toward the final end is much more dominant in Revelation. Hence it is not surprising that some interpreters have read this book as basically oriented toward the unfulfilled future. Yet the crucified and exalted Christ is a central symbol of the book, from beginning to end. Here, too, the pattern of movement to the future has been deflected by the presence of a new reality, the reality of the spirit. It is nonetheless true that the tension between present awareness and longing for the future remains at a high point; the future in no sense recedes from consciousness as it does in Acts.

If so many forces shaping the other New Testament narrative forms are also operative in the Book of Revelation, at one point there is a striking, almost total contrast. It was noted above that one of the leading features, particularly of the Gospel form but also of Acts, is the concrete particularity with which they portray and confront individual existence. The same concreteness is also characteristic of the principal New Testament narrative form which is not discussed here, namely, the parable.[7] All is different in the Apocalypse. Here there is no effort to hold the imagination to the world of concrete human existence. Except in the letters to the seven churches, the images are, with remarkable consistency, distortions and intensifications of everyday reality, "unreal," in a word, mythical. The book's concentration on the end serves to release the imagination from concrete reality; because they are pictures of the "not yet," the images are free to go their own way, rather than being conformed to concrete human existence.

The consistency of the mythical freedom of the Book of Revelation is all the more apparent when it is seen that the book is not merely free from concrete particularity in the presentation of individual existence, but also free from following the concrete course of history. This is striking since

[7]See James M. Robinson, "Jesus' Parables as God Happening," in *Jesus and the Historian: Written in Honor of Ernest Cadman Colwell*, ed. F. Thomas Trotter (Philadelphia: Westminster Press, 1968), pp. 134–50.

the usual plan of organization of an apocalyptic narrative was to present, in symbolic terms, the history of the chosen people or world history. In Daniel 10–11, for instance, the historical detail is so accurate that these chapters actually form a source for knowledge about Seleucid history. Revelation has been read this way, as a sequential, symbolic telling of history, but only with an effort can a consistent connection with history be made. The writer's vision is too free to be bound to the details of historical sequence. Many details, especially in chapters 13 and 17, may point to the Roman power, but the fact that no consensus can be reached about what Roman emperors are intended by the seven heads and ten horns of the beast (13:1; 17:7–18) is an index of the freedom of the author's imagination to transfigure historical details into symbols of cosmic struggle.

Though there is a common apocalyptic structural element to the Gospel, the history, and the apocalypse, the mythical freedom of the apocalypse raises important questions about its coherence with other forms: do they all have some similarity of function in expressing the Christian message? In spite of its lack of concreteness, the freedom of Revelation's mythical vision is limited by its relation to the figure of Christ. In both the Gospel and the history, this figure brings into question the sharp ingroup versus outgroup consciousness that is so widely characteristic of apocalyptic. In Revelation, on the other hand, the narrative strongly highlights this contrast right to the end (cf. the ominous "outside," 22:15). But even here the liturgical sections occasionally transcend this contrast (15:4; 21:3), as does the final vision (21:24; 22:2), showing that an unreflective awareness of "us" against "them" is somewhat weakened here, too, by the apprehension of a reality that calls this distinction into question.

THE USE OF SYMBOLS IN THE BOOK OF REVELATION

The methods of the writer owe little to the literary techniques of sophisticated Hellenistic culture.[8] The book is con-

[8]John W. Bowman, *The Drama of the Book of Revelation* (Philadelphia: Westminster Press, 1955), has made a sustained effort to relate the structure of the book to Greek stage. But he fails to see that rather than being dramatic scenes in which the action is advanced, the visions of Revelation are more like tableaux or individual cartoons of a comic strip, in which, one after the other, successive "scenes" are displayed.

sciously Hebraic in style, perhaps influenced by rabbinic scriptural interpretation and possibly by Jewish-Christian Gnostic speculation. The Old Testament is the great source of the author's symbolism, though he combines and revises the Old Testament symbols with so great a freedom that he almost never quotes it directly. The "invented" nature of the literary pattern is also shown by the character of the language. In general the New Testament is not favorable to a special religious language, a "sacred language." The Book of Revelation, however, approximates such a special diction, a special artistic language. It does so by imposing Hebrew or Aramaic language patterns on Greek in such a way as to produce what has been called the most sustained body of violation of the rules of Greek grammar that exists anywhere. These are not mere violations of ignorance, although it is a difficult question how much ignorance is involved. The intention, brilliantly successful, is to produce a hieratic speech, a language appropriate to a renewal of prophecy.[9]

Though it owes little or nothing to Greek drama, the book is powerfully dramatic. The basic compositional device is simple repetition—one vision set after another. It was noted above how effective this additive method is in the Gospels in leading up to the climax of the book. The same repetitive method is used in Revelation, so much so that some readers find it tedious. It is more correct to see the interwoven repetitions as building the inexorable and rapid pace of the narrative. The method of repetition, however, has been modified in two very important respects. In the first place, a common stock of symbols links the separate visions, and the repeated appearance of these symbols gives both unity and cumulative effect to the whole. "Fire," "smoke," "incense," "star," "crown," and "white" are among the basic symbols which hold these separate units together and give cumulative force as they are used in one context after another. The inter-

[9] To give one example, the liturgical phrase, "who is and who was and who is to come" (1:8, etc.) harshly violates the grammar of the Greek language (literally the second phrase runs "and he was" rather than "and who was"). Greek grammar requires that all three of the phrases be in the same construction, which in Greek would be a participle. "Who is" and "who is to come" are participles in Greek, but "who was" appears abruptly as a finite verb. This shift does take place in Hebrew. On the grammar of Revelation, see R. H. Charles, *The Revelation of St. John* (Edinburgh: T. & T. Clark, 1920), 1:cxvii–xlix.

weaving of different episodes through the use of a group of symbols running through them is a distinctive trait of this book. The Book of Daniel, for instance, which, next to Revelation, is perhaps the most carefully ordered apocalyptic book, has nothing comparable. In Daniel each vision has its own set of symbols. To take one example from Revelation, "white," a symbol of undivided wholeness and power, first appears in the white head and hair of Christ (1:14), then in the "white stone" of the eschatological initiatory rite promised to the believer in 2:17, then in a whole series of passages, most of which refer to the faithful (3:4, 5, 18; 4:4; 6:2, 11; 7:7, 13, 14; 14:14; 19:11, 14), but which culminate in the great white throne of God (20:11). The symbol thus emphasizes the common destiny of God and the faithful by its application to both; only once does it occur in connection with an evil power (6:2).[10]

The other technique by which the author achieves an interwoven texture is his use of numerical structure. Seven, the symbol of divine perfection, is the basic and recurring number. Numerous outlines have tried to show that the book is built on an outline of seven seven's.[11] This design may have been in the author's mind, but he is not bound to it in a rigid way, and he interworks his seven's with three's (the three great series of seals, bowls, and trumpets, the three woes [9:12]); four's (the four living creatures [4:6], the four-sided city [21:16]); and twelve's (the twenty-four elders, two twelve's [4:4], the twelve tribes [7:4–8], and twelve apostles and twelve gates of the city [21:12, 14]). In the outworking of the book's pattern, different numerical combinations interweave and overlap in such a way that no one outline can be taken as final.

The interweaving of visions in this numerical way, especially in the first half of the book, has the effect of combining a cyclic sense of repetition with a powerful forward thrust. The book is strongly end-oriented rather than encyclopedic

[10]Here and at other points in the study of the literary structure of Revelation I am indebted to insights of my son, William R. Beardslee.
[11]John W. Bowman, "Revelation, Book of," *Interpreter's Dictionary of the Bible* (New York: Abingdon Press, 1962), 4:64–67, presents a useful survey of the overall outline by giving his own outline and those of four other scholars.

in its mode of apocalyptic narrative, yet the repetitive structure enables it to communicate the same sense of involvement with the total human reality that the encyclopedic mode also tries to communicate.

The forward thrust of the narrative is counterbalanced in another way. From time to time, the historical-cosmic struggle is set aside by an "interlude," a vision of perfection beyond struggle (initially, and therefore not strictly as an interlude, in chapters 4–5, then in 7:1–17; 10:1–11; 14:1–5; 15:2–4; 19: 1–10). By thus repeatedly breaking through his successive cycles of struggle, the author suggests that, for the believer, the passage of time may be momentarily stopped, as he participates in advance in the total presence toward which the action moves. This double pattern of forward movement and of anticipatory penetration beyond the forward movement, is a structural expression of the tension between longing for the future and a sense of the presence of Christ and the Spirit now newly known.

The book is not turned outward toward absorbing the lore of the world, and, explicitly, the worldly reality is only taken up in judgment. But in an often unnoticed way, Revelation is open to the "world" far more deeply than any other New Testament book, namely in the sensuousness of its symbolism. In the original meaning of "aesthetic," the meaning referring to the physical impact of sensation, this is a profoundly aesthetic book. Sexual symbolism appears directly and explicitly, in both positive and negative valuations (the bride ready for her husband [19:7]; the harlot and her consorts [17:1–6, cf. esp. 17:4]). The impact of color, sound, taste, odor, and physical contact is richly communicated both in the visions of struggle and in the visions of total presence. These sensuous images have Old Testament roots. In most of the New Testament, however, the concentration on concrete human existence, and on the aspect of responsible decision in existence, has led to the bypassing of the sensuous richness which is present in the imagery of Revelation. It is not surprising that these two styles of presentation fell apart in the New Testament. Perhaps not until Dante were they successfully brought together.

APOCALYPTIC SYMBOLS AND REBELLION AGAINST STRUCTURE

In conclusion, we return to the problems of the beginning of the chapter. Historically minded theologians have reacted negatively to the Book of Revelation and have even given little attention to the study of the book during the recent debates about apocalyptic. No doubt one reason for this neglect has been the orientation of so much recent study toward the point of historical origin of Christianity; because Revelation does not come from the earliest stages, it has been neglected. In making interpretive judgments, scholars have correctly seen that a modern man cannot directly live in the symbolic world of the Book of Revelation. Hence they have tried to find nonapocalyptic forms for the expression of the total claim of apocalyptic.

At the same time, the coming of a new apocalyptic style in our day is a powerful reminder of the need for man to create a mythic space in which to live and of the kinship between the mythic space of Revelation and that of an important wing of the modern sensitivity.

Without attempting any discussion of modern apocalyptic style, it can be indicated here that a study of Revelation is relevant to it not only for the sake of understanding its historical background, but because of the book's importance as an achievement of balance between order and spontaneity.[12] The thirst for total presence tends to be destructive of order, and it was noted above that apocalyptic faith tends to reverse the original association of destructiveness with chaos and of life with order, because of its strong sense of the repressiveness of order. This motif is strong in Revelation, but the thrust toward the spontaneity of total presence is assimilated into a higher order. The remarkably structured pattern of the book, with its release of the sensuous through rapidly paced yet controlled images, maintains a tension between order and spontaneity rather than resolving the tension completely in favor of spontaneity. The spontaneity which overcomes the repressive present order is itself a higher order.

By being drawn into a structure, the dynamism and spon-

[12]On the modern apocalyptic style, see above, p. 55, note 2. Since the proverbial form is one form of expression of the modern apocalyptic style, see above, p. 31, n. 1, for further references.

taneity of the apocalyptic vision have been enabled to have a continuing cultural life. It is true that the ensuing cultural history moved far away from the original apocalyptic point of origin into a vision of a much more stable structure of existence, and that we are now witnessing a turning away from that stable vision.[13] Nonetheless, though we may postulate an ultimately "radical" apocalyptic of pure spontaneity, it is worth pondering that apocalyptic was able to make an impression on the imagination of later times in a form which kept the centrifugal, spontaneous elements in dynamic tension with centripetal, form-building elements. Whether contemporary apocalyptic style will be able to achieve a similar tension remains to be seen.

[13]Northrop Frye, *Anatomy of Criticism*, pp. 141–46, uses Revelation as the basis for his "grammar of apocalyptic imagery" in an analysis of the whole scope of archetypal imagery. His broader understanding of apocalyptic embodies both the fundamental importance of the original style and its incorporation into a more stable structure where the "end" becomes the eternal heaven.

VI

The Literary History of the
Synoptic Gospels

THE HISTORY OF THE STUDY OF THE GROWTH OF THE GOSPELS

Of all questions of literary history, the question of the synoptic Gospels has been the central one for students of the New Testament. The reason is simple: during the formative period of modern New Testament study it seemed that the answer to this question was the key to the reliability of the Christian message. During the nineteenth century most scholars, both conservative and liberal, thought that a correct historical knowledge about Jesus was an essential basis for Christian faith, even though there was no general consensus about what "historical" meant. As it became more and more clear that the Gospel of John could play at best only a marginal role in giving historical knowledge, attention focused sharply on the first three, and, while the question of literary history was studied partly for its own sake, to appreciate the Gospels and their sources in their own right, the primary motivation was the quest for an assurance that behind the Gospels was a solid core of historically accurate material about the deeds and words of Jesus.

The search for a solid basis for historical knowledge about Jesus led to a study of the literary interrelationships between the synoptic Gospels, Matthew, Mark, and Luke, for they were the sources which showed the best promise of being historical records as the nineteenth century understood these. What the relationship is, in terms of literary history, among these three books proved to be an enormously difficult prob-

64

lem, one about which it is possible to reach a decision, but one which is still being debated. Matthew, Mark, and Luke stand in some kind of close relationship, for they are very similar both in arrangement and in wording. None of them contains any statement about its relation to the others, and the "external evidence," the statements of later Christian writers about the authorship and sources of these Gospels, is so late and confusing that it is of little value in coming to understand their interrelationship. Often a good deal of weight has been laid on these ancient Christian traditions, but increasingly it appears that a judgment about the literary relationships of Matthew, Mark, and Luke must stand on the intrinsic probabilities arising from the comparison of the Gospels themselves. All of the early Christian writers were primarily concerned with the apostolic authority of the Gospels, and not in the first instance with their bare historical interrelationships. Thus the ancient Christian statement that Matthew was *written* first is basically a judgment that Matthew is the most important and most authoritative Gospel (an opinion that was also reflected in the arrangement of the books in the canon). It is very doubtful that the sources from the second century and later retained any historical memory of the actual literary interrelationships among the synoptic Gospels, or even any accurate information about their relative dates.

The basis for a decision about the mutual relationships between Matthew, Mark, and Luke must then be the nature of their actual interrelationships as revealed by a close and detailed comparative study of their structure and content. The parallels between portions of Matthew, Mark, and Luke, parallels both in content and order, are so strong that after due consideration most scholars have returned to the view (already put forth by Augustine in a special form) that there is a direct literary connection among the synoptics, that one Gospel is a literary source for another. That one or more was used by the others seems the only adequate way to explain the close relationship between them. (To explain the similarities on the basis of copying from a now-lost primitive Gospel only complicates matters by introducing an added unknown; on this line no consensus developed about what this primitive Gospel was like, for instance, whether it was shorter or longer than Mark.)

Thus the question is, what is the form of interconnection? Which book depends on which? There are some eighteen theoretical possibilities, but only a few are possible on the basis of a study of the Gospels themselves.[1] The real question is whether Matthew used Mark or Mark used Matthew. Luke cannot come first, though it has been suggested that Luke was used by Mark (Griesbach, Bleek, and Farmer). Traditionally, and especially among Roman Catholic scholars, it has been held that Matthew was the first and that Mark used Matthew, though this view has been subtly modified by some recent Catholic writers (Benoit, Vaganay), who think that the original Matthew plus Mark were in the hands of the editor of the present Matthew.

The last hundred years of study of this question have seen (1) the growth of rather general acceptance of the "priority of Mark," at least among most Protestant scholars; (2) a long period of acceptance of this view as one of the "assured results of scholarship";[2] and (3) in recent times, several important attempts to reopen the question and reestablish the priority of Matthew (Butler and Farmer).[3] The priority of Mark has usually (though not necessarily) carried with it another hypothesis, namely, that Matthew and Luke, working separately, in addition to Mark also used another (hypothetical and now lost) source, principally a collection of the words of Jesus, which came to be labeled Q. Thus the going theory has been the "two-document theory," the view that there were two basic written sources for the synoptic Gospels, Mark and Q, and that Matthew and Luke made use of both of these, but that Matthew and Luke did not know each other's work.

THE ARGUMENTS FOR AND AGAINST THE PRIORITY OF MARK

The arguments for or against the priority of Mark are of two sorts, though in actual practice the two overlap to some

[1] For a table of these possibilities, see William R. Farmer, *The Synoptic Problem*, pp. 208–9.
[2] ". . . the priority of Mark to Matthew and Luke no longer requires to be proved." James Moffatt, *An Introduction to the Literature of the New Testament* (New York: Scribner's, 1914 [3rd ed., 1922]), p. 180.
[3] B. C. Butler, *The Originality of St. Matthew* (Cambridge: Cambridge University Press, 1951); Farmer, *Synoptic Problem*.

extent. One of these is the question of order, the other the question of content. The parallels in order of units, or paragraphs, among Matthew, Mark, and Luke are very strong in the material which they have in common (Matthew and Luke have, in turn, a good deal of further material in common, the Q material mentioned above, which does exhibit many parallels of order in detail, though the overall arrangement is strikingly different in Matthew and Luke). Some of these parallels are dictated by the nature of the tradition (as the sequence betrayal, arrest, trial, crucifixion). But the close and detailed parallel of order in the common material of Matthew, Mark, and Luke is one of the strongest arguments for literary dependence among them. The usual conclusion drawn from these parallels has been that Mark probably served Matthew as a source and also was used independently by Luke. The reason for drawing this conclusion is that Matthew and Luke both follow Mark's order closely, and also, when one of them rearranges Mark's order, the other usually adheres to it.[4] Many have found this argument persuasive, but B. C. Butler and William Farmer have reversed it. They hold that the probabilities arising from order are equally strong if one supposes that Mark's order is derived from Matthew (and from Luke as well in the case of Farmer).

The argument from order was originally developed by Karl Lachmann, who, however, applied it to the hypothesis that all three synoptics were utilizing a (now-lost) primitive Gospel, which Mark reproduces most closely. Butler and Farmer hold that the argument from order loses it cogency once the hypothesis of a primitive Gospel is given up—that the parallels in order may mean something other than Markan priority if it is simply a case of interrelationships among the three. Though both argue that Matthew is in fact the earliest of the three, they differ importantly in detail: Butler argues that similarities in order between Mark and Luke are to be explained by Luke's use of Mark, while Farmer holds that Mark had access to both Matthew and Luke and followed either one or the other. This latter view has the advantage of making a more natural separation of the "Markan" from the "non-Markan" material.

It must be conceded to Farmer that, purely on the basis of

[4]Werner Georg Kümmel, *Introduction to the New Testament,* p. 46.

the statistical probability involved in rearranging blocks of material considered as separate units, the theory that Mark followed Matthew or Luke, knowing both, is as adequate as the view that Matthew and Luke each separately followed Mark. But the argument from order is not that simple. What must be asked is not only what the bare statistical probabilities are, but also how the authors may have worked. It must also be asked whether, on one view or another, there are evidences of displacement of order. Such evidences of displacement have been more adequately shown for the standard view that Mark came first than for the theory of Matthean priority held by Butler and Farmer. Thus, in Matthew 9:2, there is no evident reason for saying: "Jesus saw their faith," but when Mark's story is compared with Matthew's, it is clear that Jesus saw their faith because they had let down the paralytic through the roof.[5] Matthew has omitted this part of the story.[6] Similarly, in Matthew 4, Matthew has apparently changed Mark's "king" to "tetrarch," as the correct title for Herod Antipas, but in verse 9 returns to "king," a shift best explained by his taking the term over from Mark 6:26 and simply neglecting to make the correction in this case.[7] Similar examples can be cited from Luke.

The argument from order, considered simply in terms of the rearrangement of building blocks, is not a conclusive proof of Mark's priority. But when the shifts in order are considered in connection with the probabilities of how an author would work, the case for Mark's coming first is strengthened. Here the theory of Farmer is much more difficult than the usual theory that Mark was a source for both Matthew and Luke. Why Mark should have shifted from Matthew to Luke in determining his order never becomes clear. F. W. Beare, admittedly a proponent of the competing point of view, holds that this aspect of Farmer's work is a "total failure."[8]

The arguments from content are more complicated than those from order, because they involve a whole range of judgments about how different styles of writing and different be-

[5]Mark 2:4.
[6]Kümmel, *Introduction*, p. 48.
[7]*Ibid.*
[8]In his review of Farmer's book in the *Journal of Biblical Literature*, 84 (1965): 296.

liefs are likely to have been related to each other. These arguments are, however, more decisive and important than the question of order. Here no more than a sampling can be attempted. Evidence drawn from content may be classified under the headings of style, form, and theological concern.

As far as style is concerned, it is evident that Mark wrote in a less finished style than either of the others. All write simple, largely paratactic Greek (in which clauses are strung together with a series of "and's"). But Mark's use of this simple style is more continuous than Matthew's or Luke's.

Related to style in that details of wording are involved is the fact that in Mark there are mistakes in the recollection of the Old Testament which are "corrected" in the parallels in Matthew and Luke: Mark 1:2-3 cites as from Isaiah two passages, one from Malachi and one from Isaiah, but Matthew 3:3 and Luke 4:4-6 mention Isaiah and quote from Isaiah only, omitting the quotation from Malachi. Mark 2:26 attempts to justify picking grain on the Sabbath by mentioning David's example of eating the consecrated bread, and, in doing so, identifies David's act as having taken place when Abiathar was high priest. Matthew 12:4 and Luke 6:4 omit the reference to Abiathar, which was incorrect (according to 1 Samuel 21:1-9, Abiathar's father Ahimelech was "high priest" at this time).

It is easier to suppose that style and minor errors were improved and corrected by Matthew and Luke than to suppose that Mark introduced a less careful way of writing.

As for form, the decisions are harder to make. By the comparison of "form" is meant the comparison of the forms of the units—such as pronouncement stories and miracle stories—common to the three synoptics to see which writers present more primitive and which more developed forms. Such a comparison presupposes some standards for judging the development of forms. Butler's predominant thesis is that the semitic coloring, both of form and style, is evidence of Matthew's priority.[9] Farmer argues more sharply on form-critical grounds that Mark shows a more highly developed type of Hellenistic miracle story (with "foreign words," of special potency, for instance),[10]

[9]See, for example, Butler, *Originality*, p. 105.
[10]Mark contains a number of Aramaic words of this sort which do not appear in either Matthew or Luke: cf. Farmer, *Synoptic Problem*, pp. 172-74.

and that Mark's structure of some stories can better be understood as derived from Matthew than vice versa. For instance, Farmer holds that the parable of the wicked tenants (Mark 12:1–12) is a conflation of Matthew's and Luke's form and is shorter because it was difficult to combine the two endings which appear in Matthew and Luke.[11] But C. H. Dodd and others have persuasively argued that Matthew's conclusion is, on the contrary, an expansion and clarification of an allegorical application of the parable already present in Mark.[12]

The argument from form, particularly as Farmer develops it, presents the difficulty that, even though criteria for the development of forms in oral literature do apply in large measure to the procedures of writers of nonliterary materials, nonetheless, once the tradition is reduced to writing, other factors also come into force. It is true that in oral literature stories tend to expand, and Farmer argues that since Mark's individual stories are usually longer than Matthew's, therefore Mark has expanded Matthew's versions of these stories. But a writer like Matthew might well abridge the Marcan stories, as he is usually supposed to have done, perhaps partly to save space, while from time to time also adding further detail according to the principle of elaboration.

Thus while the argument from formal criteria is the strongest of the various arguments that can be adduced for the priority of Matthew, it is not persuasive, and other formal considerations support the priority of Mark.

A theological comparison of Matthew and Mark may include many things; here only several characteristic items can be noted. Such a comparison will readily show that Matthew's versions of parallel stories normally express a higher reverence for Jesus than Mark's do. Matthew tends not to mention human emotion expressed by Jesus, especially "negative" emotion.[13] More respect is shown toward Jesus in words addressed to

[11]*Ibid.*, pp. 248–50.
[12]C. H. Dodd, *The Parables of the Kingdom* (New York: Scribner's, 1936), pp. 124–32.
[13]Matt. 12:13, cf. Mark 3:5, "he looked around at them with anger"; Matt. 8:4, cf. Mark 1:43, "he sternly charged him"; cf. also Matt. 13:58 and Mark 6:6 (where only Mark mentions that Jesus "marveled" because of their unbelief); cf. also Matt. 19:14 and Mark 10:14. In Mark 1:34 Jesus heals "many"; in Matt. 8:16 he heals "all."

him.[14] Most striking of these differences is the reply of Jesus to the rich young man. In Mark it is, "Why do you call me good? No one is good but God alone."[15] In Matthew (after a slightly different introduction) Jesus says, "Why do you ask me about what is good?"[16] Most students have felt that it is far more understandable that Matthew has heightened the reverence expressed toward Jesus than that Mark has introduced a less respectful and more human presentation than his source. The same contrast exists between Mark and Luke, who also expresses a greater respect for Jesus in comparison to Mark.

The story of the baptism shows a related contrast; whereas in Mark the voice says, "Thou art my beloved Son; with thee I am well pleased,"[17] in Matthew the voice, more liturgically, says, "This is my beloved Son, with whom I am well pleased."[18] Probably both authors thought of the voice as a public and objective event, but the more starkly "objective" formulation of Matthew is easier to understand as a development out of Mark than vice versa.

More pervasive and less directly expressed theological contrasts abound. In general, Mark stresses the mystery and the transcendental nature of Christian faith, while Matthew presents faith as something which is "there," which is lived out in the community. The strong consensus of scholars is that Matthew's more worldly and objective understanding of faith is likely to be later than Mark's more mysterious and less objective type.

Thus, though the question of the interrelationships between Matthew, Mark, and Luke cannot be known with complete certainty, by far the most probable view is the usual one that Matthew and Luke each used Mark as a source. It simply is not the case, as both Butler and Farmer suggest, that this question has been swept under the rug for two generations. It has been constantly reexamined. There has been a steady minority of dissent from the prevailing view. Thus Adolf Schlatter, a distinguished New Testament scholar, supported the priority of

[14]Matt. 8:25, "Save, Lord; we are perishing"; compare Mark 4:38, "Teacher, do you not care if we perish?"
[15]Mark 10:18.
[16]Matt. 19:17.
[17]Mark 1:11.
[18]Matt. 3:17.

Matthew through a long career of teaching.[19] Despite the repeated presentation of the hypothesis of Matthean priority, it simply has not seemed as solid a one as the view that Mark came first, and has convinced only a few.

THE SOURCE FOR MATTHEW'S AND LUKE'S SAYINGS MATERIAL

The related question, whether or not there was a common source, Q, for the material common to Matthew and Luke that is not in Mark, is more elusive because this common source does not now exist. The "Q hypothesis" has been vigorously attacked in recent years, for instance by Butler.[20] But once the use of Mark by Matthew and by Luke has been accepted, and once it has been seen that the most probable view by far is that Luke did not use Matthew, then it becomes very likely that there was some kind of common source for the material that Matthew and Luke have in common. The similarities in the detailed sequence of the material are one compelling reason.[21] The alternate view, that Luke, though he knew Mark, also drew on Matthew, is improbable for various reasons, particularly because (1) this view does not account for the variety in the degree to which Luke and Matthew are in agreement in sections where they are parallel, (2) it does not explain his principle of selection, and (3) it does not account for his radical reordering of the larger units of discourse material, such as the Sermon on the Mount, where Matthew 5–7 is paralleled in Luke 6, 11, 12, 13, 14, and 16. Equally difficult to explain is the fact that Luke does not (except in the baptism and temptation stories) bring texts common to Matthew into the same Marcan context that Matthew does.[22]

The exact scope of the common source for Matthew and Luke is impossible to determine. It was a collection with a kerygmatic, rather than an instructional, emphasis, primarily made up of words of Jesus, and apparently it did not include a story of the death of Jesus. At some points Matthew and Luke are practically identical in detail, while at others they

[19]Cf. Adolf Schlatter, *Der Evangelist Matthäus* (6th ed.; Stuttgart: Calwer, 1963).

[20]Butler, *Originality*, esp. the first few chapters.

[21]See Vincent Taylor, "The Order of Q," *Journal of Theological Studies*, new series 4 (1953): 27–31.

[22]See Kümmel, *Introduction*, p. 50.

present very different forms of the same tradition. Probably the Q material had been written, but existed in several forms.

However, the whole course of recent study of the Gospel tradition suggests a word of caution with regard to postulating that the synoptic writers composed their books simply by following written sources. In the first century A.D. there was no sharp line drawn between written and oral tradition. Modern students have tended to think favorably of written sources because these are fixed and, therefore, supposedly dependable. But in the early years of Christian history, there seems to have been a great deal of freedom to move back and forth between written and oral tradition. Both Butler and Farmer, it should be said, are very old-fashioned at this point. The preponderance of evidence strongly suggests that Mark was known to both Matthew and Luke, both of which, however, are so different from one another that it is difficult to suppose that either knew the other. There are, however, a significant number of agreements between Matthew and Luke against Mark. Some of these may be explained by independent, parallel editing of Mark by Matthew and by Luke, some by later assimilation of one text to the other. There was a strong tendency toward such assimilation in the process of copying; usually Matthew's form, being the most familiar, was inserted into Luke and, for that matter, also into Mark in some cases. But it may also be the case that at times Matthew and Luke each drew independently on an oral tradition which was different from Mark. Taking the picture as a whole, this is far more likely than that Luke took over occasional scraps of Matthean language. There are also some passages where Matthew, and even sometimes Luke, seems to preserve an earlier form of the tradition than Mark. This need not point to the priority of Matthew, though it is not improbable that Matthew may have drawn on an oral tradition different from Mark from time to time, and it is quite possible that such tradition might in some cases represent an earlier form of the episode in question than Mark does.

Recognizing the place of oral tradition in the sources of the synoptic writers also leads one to conclude that it is difficult to identify a unified source for the material peculiar to Matthew or to Luke. At one time there was considerable enthusiasm for the theory that, in addition to Mark and Q, there was a source, sometimes called M, on which Matthew drew, and another, L, which was used by Luke. But it now seems much more probable that the materials that Matthew and Luke have which they did not draw from Mark or Q came from varied sources, largely oral.

CURRENT RESEARCH ON SYNOPTIC SOURCES

The future of synoptic literary criticism does not lie in trying to dislodge Mark from its place as the basic example of the form "Gospel." Rather it will consist in combining literary and form criticism to develop a more careful and fuller history of the stages in which the Gospels and their component sources came to be written. Important new developments in this area lie in the theory that a (partly) common "signs" source was used by Mark and John and in the attempt to uncover an early stage of the sayings source prior to Q, a stage which did not yet have a Son-of-man Christology.[23]

[23]See Robinson, "Kerygma and History in the New Testament," and Koester, "One Jesus and Four Primitive Gospels," and the references cited in these articles.

VII

Literary Criticism and
Theological Understanding

IMAGINATION AND FAITH

In this chapter we shall reflect on what it means for theology to deal with literary criticism and then note more specifically some implications for theology of the particular forms studied in the preceding chapters.

In the first place, no account of faith is adequate which fails to reckon with faith's expression in imagination and creativity. The moral and intellectual dimensions of faith have always been central to Christian theology, but too often the imaginative and creative side of faith has been suspect or ignored. The previous chapters pointed to the immense effort of imaginative vision which brought some early Christian forms of faith to expression; even from the study of the history of the synoptic Gospels discussed in the preceding chapter this should be clear, though the chapter itself was focused on a different problem. Quite apart from how it interprets the specific content of these forms of faith, an adequate theology must find a place for aesthetic creativity. For such creativity is a central component not merely in the "human response" of faith, but also in the very structure which evokes faith and thereby enables men to respond to it. From this initial point, one further step appears at once: a theology which takes imagination and creativity seriously will not be willing to limit them to functioning only in the initial stage of faith or in some uniform expression of it. Some element of spontaneity, of new vision, will have to be a possibility in the continuing history of faith.

Secondly, our study of literary form, brief as it was, has shown that the imaginative forms in which early Christianity expressed itself have roots reaching far behind the conscious concerns of that faith, linking it with the primordially religious, and it has also shown that the altered vision emerging with Christianity has had an impact reaching, again, far beyond the conscious concerns of traditional theology. Whatever the power is that works in Christian faith, it draws on roots as deep as the ancient pattern of the cultic renewal of the presence of reality, and its impact has transformed not only the shape of reality as seen by the conscious community of faith, but also the whole Western grasp of reality as well. It will be at his peril that the theologian treats any of these formative elements or consequences as side effects. Such literary-cultural background and impact may reveal the actual power (and limits) of faith more clearly than many traditional theological concerns can do.

Once these two points are granted, however, it becomes a serious question how important the original literature of early Christianity is. If the New Testament appears as part of an ongoing process of imaginative perception, important to the student of literature for its injection of certain new possibilities of vision into our history, why should not later writers have articulated these perspectives more effectively than the New Testament?

LITERATURE AS AN INDEX OF LIFE STYLE

Before confronting this question directly, it will be helpful to look more fully at a common point for dialogue between students of literature and theologians. Literary style and form are, among other things, indexes of a style of life. A particular literary style is not only appropriate to, but generative of, a life style. There is no direct correspondence between literary style and style of life, for much literature, for one thing, deals with imaginative possibilities and may explore various possibilities in one style. Besides this, no literature merely transcribes life; rather, it concentrates and intensifies it, so that its style exaggerates and distorts a style of life. It is also true that much work of the imagination, particularly in our time, tends to dissociate itself from responsibility to a particular structure of existence, a procedure which itself has implications for life style.[1] None-theless, an important and widely practiced type of literary study draws out the implications of these two styles, of litera-ture and of life, for each other.[2] At the same time, a study of style of life or structure of existence is also an important way into theology today.[3]

From the point of view of structure of existence we can ap-proach what literary study has to say about the continuing role of the New Testament in theology. The New Testament presents, in a series of expressions related to the figure of Jesus, a group of basic paradigms for the structure of Christian existence. Structurally more complex and subtly interwoven forms were produced as later expressions of Christian exis-tence. If one evaluates literature by purely formal criteria of structural complexity, it is clear that the New Testament has been surpassed by later Christian visions. But if literature be granted not just the function of bringing to expression a vision of pure form, but also a mythic power to bring the depths of existence to expression, then simple, preliterary forms like most of those in the New Testament may retain their power as paradigmatic models by virtue of their simplicity and depth, even when they have been far surpassed in technical construc-tion. The Christian community has repeatedly rediscovered the paradigmatic power of the earliest expressions of Christian existence, and students of literature are also seeing this paradig-matic power in terms of their own concerns. We may well be approaching a time when those who live in or toward Chris-tian existence will not follow the older pattern of learning about it first from the New Testament, but instead will, so to

[1]See William F. Lynch, *Christ and Apollo* (New York: New American Library, 1963 [first published 1960]), p. 64.

[2]For ancient literature, the relevance of formal style for style of life is well shown in the basic and highly form-oriented work of Eduard Norden, *Die antike Kunstprosa* (Darmstadt: Wissenschaftliche Buch-gesellschaft, 1958 [first published 1898]), 2:452–60, where he summar-izes (not for the New Testament but for the literature of developed Christianity) the shift away from individualism, cheerfulness, national and class exclusiveness, and concern for formal beauty as characteristic of the shift in life style reflected in the forms of Christian literature as compared with what preceded them.

[3]See John B. Cobb, Jr., *The Structure of Christian Existence* (Philadel-phia: Westminster Press, 1967); Jack Boozer and William A. Beardslee, *Faith to Act: An Essay on the Meaning of Christian Existence* (New York: Abingdon Press, 1967); William Hamilton, *The New Essence of Christianity* (New York, Association Press, 1962).

speak, work their way back to the New Testament from other models. It is nonetheless still true that the cluster of paradigms centering around the figure of Jesus bring the structure of Christian existence to expression with a simplicity, power, and depth that will keep the New Testament in a central place wherever men are concerned for Christian existence.

THE VITALITY OF THE CHRISTIAN VISION

The real question is not whether the New Testament can maintain its place as the basic cluster of paradigms of Christian existence, but whether the Christian vision of existence is itself exhausted. Not only the rejection of traditional Christian intellectual formulations, but also a far-reaching shift of symbolic values, testifies to the profound transformation of sensibility which is taking place in our time. To take only one simple example, the symbol of "whiteness," an ancient light symbol which links the believer with God in the Book of Revelation, becomes a negative symbol of death and repression in such important modern writers as William Blake and Herman Melville. This symbolic shift is directed toward separating the symbols of order and controlling power from the symbols of life. It is thus connected with the breakdown in the conventional narrative structure which was founded on the victory of order-life over chaos-death. The Christian structure of existence has always been understood as standing within this ancient dialectic, and, if the latter is dissolved in favor of an apocalyptic style which is uncommitted to any center of meaning and value, it is a question whether a Christian style of existence could still function.

There are those who greet this shift in sensibility by a radical interpretation of Christian eschatology as a total reversal whereby the meaning of ultimacy ("God," "Christ," and the "other world") is shifted wholly into the realm of immanence ("this world"), and the pole of order is visualized as disappearing in the spontaneity of the apocalyptic transformation.[4] Such a radical Christian vision has real contact with motifs in early Christian apocalyptic eschatology. But the radical or death-of-

[4]See Thomas J. J. Altizer, *The Gospel of Christian Atheism* (Philadelphia: Westminster Press, 1966).

God eschatology presupposes that the future hope of early Christianity contains a hatred of the past which in fact it does not contain. Rather the past, and hence structures of order, are taken up into the future, and this means that order is an element in life. While we cannot predict how the shift in our cultural sensibility will come out, nor yet see all that is implied in it, it is clear that it cannot be met simply by an affirmation of tradition. Engagement with the experience of chaos in the modern world will also transform the Christian vision. Yet it is precisely at such a juncture that imaginative reentry into the paradigmatic early expressions of Christian existence becomes of basic importance, for (as we have tried to show) in these expressions the pressure of new vitality and life thrusts to break the bonds of order. But in the New Testament faith, in the expressions which were able to endure, power was enabled to become life-giving precisely by entering into structure, not abolishing order but transforming it. The transformed order was not timeless but was rather a historical order from which sprang such basic elements in the early Christian vision as the concreteness of grasp of individual existence discussed in connection with the Gospels. Unless an analogous fusion of vitality with historical order can be recaptured in our own time, the prospects for a continuation of Christian existence are not good.

A final general point is that our discussion has emphasized the affinity of early Christian forms with their mythic roots and holds that it is an illusion to believe that the mythic-imaginative dimension can be ignored by modern faith. At the same time, it is not possible for modern man to live in the archaic mythical world, and the question of how to deal with the mythic dimension is an urgent one for theology and a question that has not been adequately met. The New Testament itself displays a double stance toward myth, both breaking and criticizing existing mythic structures and expressing its vision in forms which contain mythical elements.[5] In the present, very different world, something analogous is required. That is, contemporary men will not be able to enter into an integral world of myth, but fragmented mythical structures, both traditional

[5] Wilder, *Language of the Gospel*, p. 129.

and freshly minted, will continue to be indispensable to them for expressing their vision of faith. In the literary field something similar is suggested by Northrop Frye's analysis of the succession of "modes" in Western literature. He notes a historical progression away from myth in a series from the mythical mode through romance and the high and low mimetic modes to the ironic mode, but observes that strongly mythical themes reappear in the ironic mode.[6] It should be added that this point is in no way intended to suggest that the mythic imagination should be exempt from rational and moral criticism, for one of the prominent features of our world is the emergence of demonic myth.

IMPLICATIONS OF THE NARRATIVE FORM
FOR THEOLOGICAL INTERPRETATION

Finally, we shall indicate briefly some ways in which specific New Testament literary structures can cast light on some contemporary theological issues.

An attempt to draw general conclusions from the brief studies in this book is bound to be one-sided, for the topics chosen here are not fully representative of New Testament literary criticism. With the exception of the proverb, all the forms studied above are large forms of whole books: the Gospel, the history, the apocalypse. Most New Testament literary criticism deals with shorter units such as the parable and the other synoptic forms or the liturgical poems in the epistles. Many have believed that these shorter forms are closer to the theological core of early Christianity. At least of the synoptic forms, such as parable and apophthegm, it can be said that they do engage the reader or hearer in a direct confrontation. It is no accident that the first form discussed by Wilder is "the dialogue."[7] The dialogical confrontation of the reader by the parable has become the model for a whole approach to the language of faith, summed up in the phrase of Ernst Fuchs, "one does not interpret the parables, the parables interpret him."[8] The analysis of the proverb given above showed that this form, as used in

[6]Frye, *Anatomy of Criticism*, pp. 34–35, 42. Kafka and Joyce are his examples of the point.
[7]Wilder, *Language of the Gospel*, chap. 3.
[8]See Robert W. Funk, *Language, Hermeneutic, and the Word of God* (New York: Harper & Row, 1966), chap. 3 and p. 16, with references to the work of Fuchs.

the discourse material of the synoptic Gospels, functioned in this same dialogical way. The affinity between these brief synoptic forms and the existentialist theology is clear, for this theology concentrates on the moment of freedom and decision.

At the same time, we have shown how, when a larger framework of meaning is required, the narrative or story is typically chosen.[9] Wilder, too, has emphasized how characteristic of the New Testament the story form is.[10]

Our interpretation of the narrative has emphasized that, while it does play a role in confrontation, it functions as well to show the reader who he is, by setting him in a larger dynamic framework. The story tells him where he has come from and where he is going; one can say that whereas sheer confrontation is an alteration of identity, the story enables one to find a continuing identity. It has the further possibility of showing the hearer how he can take part in the story itself, of enlisting his work and creativity. In theological terms, the confrontational role of the proverb and parable are easily interpreted by the model of "justification by faith," while the story embodies other elements that cannot easily be fitted into this model. The basic theological question which an understanding of the larger narrative styles places before contemporary New Testament theology is the question of the adequacy of the basic model, justification by faith, which has dominated not only the existentialist theology, but also the new hermeneutic which has grown out of it. This is a powerful and central model, and one which is not to be superseded in expressing the receptivity, the sense of gift, which is at the heart of Christian existence. Yet, by itself, it is not able to express either the positive relation to the past, so evident in the celebration of the past in Gospel and history, nor the enlistment of the self in creativity and work toward the future which these forms also display. As Wilder says, "Man is made to share in the works of God and not only in his love."[11]

[9]One very important New Testament form, the letter, is obviously in a different category. A valuable recent treatment of the letter, dealing with its literary form and relating it to the phenomenology of language, is in Funk, *Language*, chaps. 9–11.

[10]Wilder, *Language of the Gospel*, chap. 4; Wilder is thinking, however, primarily of briefer narrative forms.

[11]Amos N. Wilder, "The Word as Address and the Word as Meaning," in Robinson and Cobb, eds., *New Hermeneutic*, p. 202.

THE SYMBOLIZATION OF HOPE

Since the specific forms into which the dynamic of New Testament faith is cast are forms which take the passage of time into the future seriously,[12] literary study would point toward the importance, for theology, of hope and the future, which, on other grounds, are now becoming so central in theology.

The symbolization of hope in the New Testament is strongly centered on the image of the final end. The end carries the meaning of totality, of total presence, yet the very effort to give faith a form in which it can be communicated holds total presence at a distance, as it becomes one element in the tension of form and dynamic. The tension between the total presence signified by the end and Christian existence as a continuing identity formed by movement to the future cannot be resolved by literary study alone. But even those who cannot incorporate a final end into their own theologies can recognize the immense service rendered to theology by the quite varied thinkers who have kept in theology the sense of movement from past to future toward realization, by relating Christian existence to the end.[13] This is the central point conveyed by the future-oriented literary structures of the New Testament. As Sam Keen puts the meaning of hope in a contemporary theological context:

> Although the categories of experience yield evidence that is at best ambiguous and is sometimes indicative of the finality of death and the triumph of evil, I *nevertheless* decide to trust that there is a deathless source of human life in which the meaning created within human history is conserved and brought to fulfillment.[14]

Though the model of justification by faith is not wide enough to express all that belongs to the structure of Christian existence

[12]The Gospel of John is an exception at this point.
[13]For strikingly different interpretations of the end, see Oscar Cullmann, *Christ and Time,* trans. F. V. Filson (rev. ed.; Philadelphia: Westminster Press, 1962); Wolfhart Pannenberg, in James M. Robinson and John B. Cobb, Jr., eds., *Theology as History* (New York: Harper & Row, 1967); Pierre Teilhard de Chardin, *The Future of Man,* trans. Norman Denny (New York: Harper & Row, 1964). Jürgen Moltmann, *Theology of Hope,* trans. James W. Leitch (New York: Harper & Row, 1967), operates predominantly with the more open concept of "future."
[14]Sam Keen, "Hope in a Post-Human Era," in Martin E. Marty and Dean G. Peerman, eds., *New Theology No. 5* (New York: Macmillan, 1968), p. 88.

set forth in the basic New Testament paradigms, another unitary model of Christian existence is not proposed here. It seems more likely that a cluster of models, rather than a unitary conceptualization, is indicated at least for the time being. This would be in keeping with early Christianity, which in the New Testament expressed its faith in a cluster of patterns, related, on one level, by the effort to express what was understood to be a common style of life and, on another level, by a common relation to Christ. Hence it is not necessary to look for one basic literary structure (confrontation or narrative) which will be taken as *the* fundamental Christian form, but it is important for theology to bring to expression the group of motifs expressed in the various forms. Such a procedure would also make room for the continuing place of new creative vision, while still allowing for the critical function of the basic New Testament paradigms of Christian existence.

Glossary

ESCHATOLOGY, ESCHATOLOGICAL. The understanding of the final goal or consummation of existence; originally signifying a specifically religious vision, the term is often used today more broadly to describe visions of the breakup of existing order.

EXISTENTIALISM, EXISTENTIAL. The view that man has no essence or nature imposed on him, but that he constitutes himself by his free choices.

FORM CRITICISM. The study of the history and function of the forms in which a message (and specifically the message about Jesus) is communicated.

GNOSTICISM. A faith approximately contemporaneous with early Christianity, and at times interpenetrating with it, which held that man's goal was to escape from concrete existence and be rejoined with the godhead.

HERMENEUTICS. The study and practice of interpreting literature or faith from one historical context in another.

KERYGMATIC. In the style of preaching or proclamation, whereby the hearer or reader is personally confronted.

MYTH, MYTHOLOGICAL. Myth, originally the story or speech associated with cult, expresses an understanding of existence. It relates man's existence to the universe by means of an unreflective participation which is not possible for modern men, but abundant fragments or elements of myth remain in contemporary life, and many think that some form of myth is essential for the formation of a human world.

PHENOMENOLOGY OF RELIGION AND LANGUAGE; PHENOMENOLOGICAL. The study of the forms appearing to consciousness, with attention to their intention, but disregarding their claim to reality.

PRIMORDIAL. "Original," in the sense of that surpassing reality which is the *origin* of transient reality.

Q. The label for a collection of sayings or "logia" of Jesus. Many scholars suppose that such a collection was used by Matthew and Luke, but the collection itself does not now exist.

TEXTUAL CRITICISM. The study of the varieties of wording in the various copies of a writing, to determine the relationships among the variations, and, if possible, the earliest or original form.

TRADITION. The formalized memory which embodies a community's pattern of thought and action.

84

Annotated Bibliography

ALONSO-SCHÖKEL, LUIS. *The Inspired Word: Scripture and Tradition in the Light of Language and Literature.* Translated by Francis Martin. New York: Herder & Herder, 1965. A fine introduction to the literary study of the Bible with considerable emphasis on the philosophy of language. The concrete data are taken almost entirely from the Old Testament.

AUERBACH, ERICH. *Mimesis: The Representation of Reality in Western Literature.* Translated by Willard Trask. Garden City: Doubleday Anchor Books, 1957. First published in English, 1953. A penetrating discussion of how style has been shaped by perception of reality. A basic book for students of the literary influence of biblical faith.

BULTMANN, RUDOLF. *The History of the Synoptic Tradition.* Translated by John Marsh from the 3rd revised German edition. New York: Harper & Row, 1963. An indispensable work for literary study. Though it concentrates on form criticism, it is rich in insight into artistic form and religious function.

———. *Theology of the New Testament.* Translated by Kendrick Grobel. 2 vols.; New York: Scribner's, 1951–55. A fundamental work for New Testament studies. Though not directly concerned with literary criticism, this book is important for literary studies, because it shows how the fundamental questions of interpretation are seen by an existentialist theology.

FARMER, WILLIAM R. *The Synoptic Problem.* New York: Macmillan, 1964. A significant attempt to overturn the usual "two document" theory of the sources of the synoptic Gospels. The book contains a valuable, though incomplete, history of the scholarly debate on this question. For reasons set forth in the text of this book, Farmer's effort has not been widely accepted.

FRYE, NORTHROP. *Anatomy of Criticism.* New York: Atheneum, 1967. First published, 1957. A basic work of literary criticism, important for students of the New Testament both for the breadth of its vision and for its understanding of the role of myth in literature.

FUNK, ROBERT W. *Language, Hermeneutic, and the Word of God.* New York: Harper & Row, 1966. A pioneering exploration of New Testament interpretation in the context of modern views of linguistic analysis and hermeneutic.

HOPPER, STANLEY R., and MILLER, DAVID L., eds. *Interpretation: The Poetry of Meaning.* New York: Harcourt, Brace & World, 1967. Essays which probe at a number of frontiers of the theory of interpretation.

KOESTER, HELMUT. "One Jesus and Four Primitive Gospels." *Harvard Theological Review* 41(1968): 203–47. A presentation of the growing edge of historical scholarship on the Gospels, showing how in actual study form criticism, literary criticism, and redaction criticism all interact.

KÜMMEL, WERNER GEORG. *Introduction to the New Testament.* Translated by A. J. Mattill, Jr. from the 14th edition. New York: Abingdon Press, 1966. Sometimes referred to as Feine-Behm-Kümmel from the authors of the earlier editions. A thorough and up-to-date discussion of the content and historical development of the New Testament books. Particularly detailed on the history of the synoptic Gospels. Contains an extensive bibliography.

ROBINSON, JAMES M., and COBB, JOHN B., JR., eds. *The New Hermeneutic.* New Frontiers in Theology, vol. 2. New York: Harper & Row, 1964. A discussion between German and American scholars about the perspective from which one interprets a faith expressed in one historical situation in another.

VIA, DAN O., JR. *The Parables: Their Literary and Existential Dimension.* Philadelphia: Fortress Press, 1967. A book which breaks new ground by looking at the parables as "aesthetic objects" or works of art. Via's important new insights lead him to undervalue the extent to which aesthetic perception is embedded in historical circumstance.

WELLEK, RENÉ, and WARREN, AUSTIN. *Theory of Literature.* 3rd ed. New York: Harcourt, Brace & World, 1962. A thorough and systematic introduction to the various methods of studying literature.

WILDER, AMOS N. *The Language of the Gospel: Early Christian Rhetoric.* New York: Harper & Row, 1964. At present the basic work on the literary art of the New Testament, important for its study of oral forms and for its insight into the novelty of New Testament speech.